A SAINSBURY COOKBOOK

LOW-FAT
COOKERY

COOKING AND EATING FOR HEALTH AND FITNESS

WENDY GODFREY

CONTENTS

Published exclusively for J Sainsbury plc
Stamford House Stamford Street
London SE1 9LL
by Martin Books
Simon & Schuster Consumer Group
Grafton House 64 Maids Causeway
Cambridge CB5 8DD

ISBN 0 85941 512 0

First published 1985
Eighth impression July 1992

Text, photographs and illustrations
©J Sainsbury plc 1985, 1992

Printed in Italy by Printer Trento

THE AUTHOR

Wendy Godfrey was born in Kent, but spent most of her school life in the Midlands. She developed her interest in food and cookery at an early age. After Domestic Science College in Gloucester she taught for seven years and then changed to the food manufacturing industry, as a Home Economist. She subsequently became Senior Home Economist at Sainsbury's, where she is currently in the Marketing Department.

Wendy is the author of several books on food and cookery, including the Sainsbury Guides *Food and Health* and *Cheese*.

Wendy lives in London, with her husband and three sons.

INTRODUCTION

This book is written mainly for those people who would like to make sensible eating a part of a generally healthy lifestyle. The emphasis is obviously on cutting down fat consumption, particularly saturated fat consumption (page 10), but the whole subject must be put in perspective. Fat is still a valuable source of energy and *should not be cut out altogether*. There are, however, several helpful techniques and rules to follow which will significantly reduce your habitual intake of fat, and they will all be found in the

book. The recipes also follow other current nutritional guidelines: they are high in dietary fibre, with one or two exceptions low in sugar, and also low in salt. The latter is an ingredient which can be cut down drastically, and I have tried to flavour the dishes in other ways. You can always add a little salt at the table if you feel it is necessary. If you have found it easy to give up sugar in hot drinks, you will find it just as easy to reduce salt intake.

A selection of accompaniments to a low-fat meal of Consommé with Citrus Zest, Smoked Haddock Pie with vegetables and fresh fruit.

Eating and health

Never a week goes by without a newspaper or magazine publishing an article on eating for good health. Two major publications have precipitated most recent articles: the COMA (Committee on Medical Aspects of Food Policy) report on diet and cardiovascular disease, and the NACNE (National Advisory Committee on Nutritional Education) discussion document. Although differing in detail, the general nutritional message of both is the same. On average, our consumption of fats, sugars and salt should be decreased, and our intake of dietary fibre increased.

Nutrition never has been and never will be an exact science, because there are so many variables involved, and their interaction is very complex. For this reason it is very difficult to isolate one variable and examine its impact even over a generation, because so many factors such as smoking, excess weight, lack of exercise and stress can affect the general level of health. It is a fact, though, that the United Kingdom has one of the world's highest death rates from heart disease. A horrifying statistic is that 40 per cent of men and 38 per cent of women will suffer or die from coronary heart disease. The group most at risk is men in their 40s. A great deal of the medical evidence produced so far suggests that reducing our fat intake would be a major step in reducing heart disease. The COMA report suggests a reduction by the end of the century of 17 per cent so that fats provide about 35 per cent of our energy intake, instead of the current 40 per cent. The NACNE recommendations go even further and suggest that fat should account for only 30 per cent of our energy intake by the year 2000. It is useful here to point out that *energy intake* is very different from *food intake*. Fat provides just over twice as many kilocalories (or kiloJoules) weight for weight as proteins or carbohydrates; that is, fat gives you just over twice as much energy as the same amount of protein or carbohydrates.

Recommendations such as these can only be

implemented slowly. It is not like taking up a crash diet, from which you expect results within a short length of time. They imply a fairly fundamental shift in eating habits, which should begin in childhood, so that healthy eating becomes a habit in later life. Nevertheless an adult making a serious attempt to adhere to sensible nutritional guidelines can radically improve his or her health.

Although this book is mainly about fat, it is helpful to look at some of the other factors which together can promote general good health.

On the dietary side, the recommendation is also to cut down our consumption of sugar and salt. Some experiments have shown that there is a correlation between intake of salt and high blood-pressure or hypertension. How many times have you seen people sprinkle salt indiscriminately over their meal? In most cases this is before they have tasted the food to judge the level of seasoning. Salt can be given up gradually in the same way as sugar, and after a while any over-salting of food seems quite unpleasant. You will find that hardly any recipes in this book have salt in the ingredients list. This is because it is preferable to find out by tasting whether any additonal salt is necessary at all; especially when the dish is well-flavoured or spiced with other ingredients.

Although we are advised to increase consumption of carbohydrates, this advice is, of course, mainly directed to starches and not sugars, and particularly those starchy foods which contain fibre, such as cereals and pulses. The other carbohydrate group, sugars, is one of the contributory factors in dental caries, and it is particularly recommended, besides a general sugar reduction, to restrict sugar intake between meals.

Dietary fibre has been the nutritional hero of the last decade, and this is the one area of consumption in our diet that should be increased. There is a possible connection between lack of dietary fibre and diseases and conditions common in western societies such as constipation, diverticulitis and cancer of the colon, and the fibre message seems already to be having an effect on eating patterns. More wholemeal bread is eaten than ever before and there is also a swing away from traditional breakfast cereals to the high-fibre variety. Vegetarianism, with its relatively high intake of fibre from fruit and vegetables is also increasingly popular.

A sensible diet keeping to the guidelines already described is not the only way to promote good health. Other factors may be equally important. The evidence linking smoking with many respiratory and heart diseases is so great that it cannot be ignored. One of the hazards, though, of giving up smoking is that the appetite increases. It therefore needs double the will-power, both to stop smoking and to reduce food intake, or at least to keep it stable.

It may surprise you to find that alcohol provides energy. Though it is not commonly regarded as a food, 1 g of alcohol in fact releases 7 kilocalories. The problems concerned with excessive intake are not only medical but also economic and social. Guidelines are for the average daily quantity not to exceed 4 per cent of energy intake which is the equivalent to just under a pint of beer or quarter of a bottle of wine.

One only has to look at the multitude of dance studios and gymnasia which have sprung up all over the country to realise that the idea of the benefits of exercise has really caught on. There are many theories about what sort of exercise is most beneficial, some promoting 'heavy' exercise for short periods, and others regular, gentle exercise. It is up to individuals to find a routine which works for them. The regular exercise started at school in physical education lessons should certainly be carried on throughout life. Even those in retirement can still join in an activity like ballroom dancing, and take regular, brisk walks.

Hardly anyone actually enjoys being under stress, and it is widely recognised that an over-stressful lifestyle can lead to illness. It is difficult, however, to give guidelines on how to reduce stress, as lifestyles vary so much. There are certain personal events which are known to be stressful, such as marriage, divorce, death in the family, changing job, moving house. In addition, many jobs expose employees to high stress levels; men in their 40s are particularly vulnerable. It is a good idea to be aware of the danger at these times, and to concentrate on all the other factors which promote good health. Whatever the stresses and worries of everyday life, it is helpful to find some way to relax and unwind from them. It may be just watching television, especially if you have a particularly active job, but those with sedentary jobs might find it better to take up some sort of sport.

Following all of the guidelines should increase the overall feeling of well-being, but there is evidence to suggest that even just changing your diet to one with less fat is going to improve and maintain your general good health.

The role of fat in the diet

If it is the general consensus of opinion that eating less fat is beneficial, why do we need fat at all? Many years ago, nutritionists grouped fats together as 'body warmers'. This is because fat converts into energy in the body, and releases more energy than other foods. Furthermore, fat releases energy more slowly, as it takes longer to be digested and absorbed.

Energy is measured in kilocalories, commonly known as calories but if you travel to countries where all measurements are metric you will find that energy is measured in kiloJoules. The conversion rate is 4.2 kiloJoules = 1 kilocalorie. Carbohydrates, proteins and fats all provide energy, but fat supplies more than twice as much energy, weight for weight, as other foods.

A reasonable approximation is:

1 gram of protein releases 4 kilocalories

1 gram of carbohydrate releases 4 kilocalories

1 gram of fat releases 9 kilocalories

Everyone needs energy to keep warm, to move about, and for basic body functions like breathing. The main problem is to keep the balance correct, and to eat only enough food to provide the energy which will be expended. Excess energy is converted into fat and laid down in the body tissues, with the result that you gain weight.

Fat is made up of a number of fatty acids, some of which are essential for formation of body cells. These are divided into three groups, according to their molecular structure.

Saturated fatty acids
(called saturated fats)

These are mainly found in food from animal sources and are the ones, which, if eaten in excess, may contribute to increased levels of cholesterol in the blood (see page 11).

Sources: butter, cream, whole milk, cheese, meat fat, dripping, lard, suet, margarines not specified as polyunsaturates, coconut and palm oils, cocoa and chocolate.

Mono-unsaturated fatty acids

Although these add to the daily fat intake, they have no effect on the cholesterol levels in the blood. Some of the foods in which they are found also contain saturated fatty acids.

Sources: Olive oil, groundnut oil, olives, avocados. Oily fish such as herring, mackerel and salmon.

Polyunsaturated fatty acids

These are the fatty acids which can lower the blood cholesterol level. The oils in which they are found also contain mono-unsaturated and saturated fats.

Sources: mainly liquid oils from plant seeds – safflower, sunflower, corn (maize) and soyabean. The most polyunsaturated oil is safflower which contains 72% 'poly' and the rest 'mono' and saturated. It is possible to buy soft margarines which are as high as 50% 'poly'.

Cholesterol

Cholesterol has the reputation of being a nutritional 'nasty', but much research work is being done to find out at what stage, and at what concentration in the body it becomes a matter for concern.

It is a fat-like substance, which is transported round the body in the bloodstream, and is needed for the formation of some hormones. Enough is produced naturally in our bodies for our needs so we do not need extra cholesterol from food. Over a period of years, fatty deposits tend to build up naturally in the arteries. A high cholesterol level in the blood speeds up this process as the excess cholesterol accumulates, making the arteries narrower and narrower and increasing the likelihood of a heart attack. This happens when a narrowed artery in the heart muscle itself is blocked by a blood clot travelling in the bloodstream, thus preventing blood getting to the heart to give it the oxygen it needs.

A high-fat diet is likely to increase the cholesterol level in the blood, although there are other factors involved. Research shows that reducing the intake of saturated fatty acids, or, to a lesser extent, substituting polyunsaturates for saturates, tends to decrease the blood cholesterol level.

All foods from plant or vegetable sources are completely cholesterol-free. Those foods high in cholesterol are egg yolk, lamb and chicken liver, kidneys, some shellfish, cream, butter and cheese, particularly Stilton and Cheddar. Although it is important not to eat too much of these cholesterol-rich foods, it is far more important to cut down on all foods containing saturated fat, and also to be aware of other ways to reduce the risk of heart disease, such as stopping smoking, taking plenty of exercise and avoiding stressful situations.

Sainsbury's sell a comprehensive range of oils and margarines, suitable for all cooking requirements. This table shows the sources of these oils and fats, and their calorific value per 100 g.

'Hydrogenation' is a manufacturing process by which liquid oils and fats are made solid. This information was correct at the time of going to press.

OILS		
Type	*Source*	*Calories per 100 g*
Olive	olives	900
Groundnut	groundnuts	900
Sunflower	sunflower seed	900
Safflower	safflower seed	900
Corn	maize	900
Soya	soya bean	900
Blended vegetable	soya bean and rapeseed	900
FATS		
Block Margarine	palm oil, rapeseed hydrogenated fish oil	730
Soft Margarine	hydrogenated fish oil, soya	730
Luxury Soft Margarine	hydrogenated fish oil, rapeseed, palm	730
Sunflower Margarine	sunflower, safflower, hydrogenated soya/palm	730
Soya Margarine	soya, hydrogenated soya, palm	730
Low-fat Spread	soya, hydrogenated soya/palm	360

HOW TO CUT DOWN ON FAT

'Bread and butter' is a phrase often used metaphorically to stand for the basis of all needs. 'Bread and soft margarine high in polyunsaturates' does not have the same ring about it, and yet it would be a far better basis of our dietary needs. Even better would be bread alone – and wholemeal bread at that!

It may surprise you to know how many foods do contain fat – cakes, biscuits, pastries, snacks and potato crisps, mayonnaise and salad cream, British and Continental sausages, nuts, pizzas and ice cream to name only a selection. Then there are the obvious fats – butter, margarine,

The same amount of energy, 450 kilocalories, is released from 4.76 oz (119 g) pasta (a carbohydrate food), from 13.32 oz (333 g) trout (a low-fat protein food) and from only 2 oz (50 g) oil (which is 100% fat).

suet, oils, cream, cheese, fat on meat and bacon, whole milk. It is probably easy looking at this list to see where fats in your diet can be cut down.

In the UK, Sainsbury's were the pioneers of the fresh skimmed and semi-skimmed milk called Vitapint. Skimmed milk is now gaining in popularity as customers become more diet and health conscious. It represents a reduction in fat of between 1.6 g and 3.7 g per 100 g compared with fresh, pasteurised whole milk which has 3.8 g fat per 100 g.

Below I have given lower fat substitutes for many everyday components of our diet.

Butter for spreading

☐ Use a low-fat spread, or a margarine which is high in polyunsaturates. Even better, eat bread and crackers on their own!

Butter or lard for frying

☐ Use vegetable oils which are high in polyunsaturates or vegetable fats.
☐ Grill bacon, sausages, burgers and other meat products wherever possible instead of frying them, so that some excess fat drains away.
☐ Fry sausages, bacon and meat without fat in a good non-stick pan. (Sometimes, excess fat can even be drained away after cooking.)
☐ If you must eat chips, have large, plain-cut ones, not the crinkle-cut type which have a much larger surface area through which to absorb fat.

Full-fat cheese

☐ Substitute the half-fat cheeses:
11% fat cheese – half the fat of Cheddar
14% fat cheese – half the fat of Edam
17% fat blue cheese – half the fat of Danish Blue
14% fat cheese is also available ready-grated for cooking.
☐ Eat fresh fruit instead of having a cheese course.

Cream cheese

☐ Use skimmed milk soft cheese, fromage frais, quark or half-fat creamery cheese instead. Cottage cheese, although low in fat, is also available in half fat varieties.

Whole milk

☐ Substitute semi-skimmed or skimmed milk such as Vitapint, or a long-life equivalent, or skimmed milk powder made up with water.
☐ Drink tea with lemon instead of milk. This is ideal for delicately flavoured teas like Earl Grey.
☐ Drink black coffee to appreciate the full flavour of the beans.
☐ Drink fresh fruit juices or mineral water as a change from hot beverages.

Cream

☐ Use natural or vanilla-flavoured yogurt or fromage frais on desserts and in cooking, for example Pork with Apricots (page 46).
☐ Make a vegetable purée for savoury dishes, for example, Lamb Fillet with Leek Purée and Rosemary Sauce (page 38).
☐ Use fresh fruit purée as a sauce for desserts, instead of cream or custard.
☐ Try eating desserts without accompaniments to appreciate their flavour.
☐ Substitute interesting fresh fruit, or dried fruit salad cooked without sugar for prepared desserts, to gain the benefits of fibre with almost no added fat.

Meat and Poultry

☐ Look out for Sainsbury's extra-trimmed meat. The maximum fat content is declared on the label. There are choices for lamb, pork, beef and veal.
☐ Young birds have less fat than boiling fowl (casserole hens). Turkey and skinless chicken joints have the lowest fat content of any poultry.
☐ Kidney, liver, venison, rabbit, hare and other game are relatively low in fat.
☐ Other ingredients in meat dishes should be as low in fat as possible.
☐ Use beans or pulses as a low-cost, low-fat protein alternative.

STARTERS

When choosing a starter for a low-fat meal, pick a fatless main ingredient; fruit and vegetables are both ideal as a base. There are some obvious choices for a simple starter – melon, grapefruit, strips of raw vegetables with a cottage cheese dip. Canned consommé also makes a good basis for many varieties of clear soup with shredded vegetables as a garnish. Some of the recipes in this section are more substantial and would be better followed by a light main course.

Cucumber Boats

Secret Mousse

Spinach and Butter Bean Soup

SPINACH AND BUTTER BEAN SOUP

One serving has 65 kilocalories and 2 g fat   Serves 6

Preparation time 15 minutes + 15 minutes cooking

1 tablespoon (15 ml spoon) sunflower oil

2 cloves of garlic, crushed

6 oz (175 g) young spinach

7¾ oz (211 g) can of butter beans

1¾ pints (1 litre) chicken stock

To garnish:

julienne strips of lemon rind (optional)

The butter beans add a nutty flavour to the soup, as well as thickening it. Other green vegetables could be used instead of spinach, for example, brussels sprouts are particularly good.

Heat the oil in a pan, and soften the garlic in it. Add the spinach and butter beans with liquid from the can and ½ pint (300 ml) of the stock. Simmer for 15 minutes, then blend, sieve, or put through a food processor. Add the remaining stock and reheat. Garnish with strips of lemon rind if you like, and serve fairly soon, as the soup will lose colour if left to stand.

SECRET MOUSSE

One serving has 43 kilocalories and less than 1 g fat   Serves 6

Preparation time 10 minutes + chilling

8 oz (227 g) carton of skimmed milk soft cheese

14½ oz (411 g) can of beef consommé

2 cloves of garlic, crushed

½–1 teaspoon (2.5 ml–5 ml spoon) garam masala

6 coriander leaves

I made this dish often several years ago, and no one could ever guess what the ingredients were. The skimmed milk soft cheese now replaces the cream cheese previously used, and although the texture is creamy, there is less than 1 g of fat in each serving.

Blend the cheese, half of the can of consommé, the garlic and the garam masala together. (This can best be done in a mixer or food processor.) Pour into six individual dishes. Chill in the refrigerator until set (about 1 hour). Put a coriander leaf on top of each. Warm the remaining consommé until liquid, spoon over each mousse and chill again for about half an hour. Serve with rye bread or wholemeal toast.

CUCUMBER BOATS

One serving has 80 kilocalories and 3 g fat   Serves 6

Preparation time 40 minutes

2 cucumbers

12 oz (375 g) carton of
cottage cheese

2 teaspoons (2 × 5 ml
spoon) concentrated mint
sauce

To garnish:

paprika pepper

shredded lettuce or mint
leaves

*A summer starter to make when cucumbers are
plentiful. Fresh mint can be used instead of the
concentrated mint sauce.*

Cut the cucumbers in half, and then cut 3 of the
halves lengthways, giving 6 pieces. Scoop out
the seeds from the 6 'boats'. Blend the cottage
cheese with the mint sauce, and pile this mixture
into the boats.

Peel the remaining half a cucumber, and then
with the peeler take long thin slices from the
outside. Sprinkle the boats with paprika pepper.
Pleat the strips of cucumber to form the 'waves'
around the boats, with the shredded lettuce or
mint leaves as a garnish.

CHINESE PANCAKES

One serving has 210 kilocalories and 3 g fat   Serves 6

Preparation time 1 hour

For the pancakes:

8 oz (225 g) plain flour

½ pint (300 ml) water

1 teaspoon (5 ml spoon)
sunflower oil

For the filling:

4 oz (100 g) beansprouts

a bunch of spring onions,
trimmed and sliced
lengthways

8 oz (227 g) can of water-
chestnuts, drained and sliced

1-inch (2.5 cm) piece of root
ginger, peeled and very
finely chopped

4 tablespoons (4 × 15 ml
spoon) hoisin sauce

2 tablespoons (2 × 15 ml
spoon) dry sherry

*The only time I have eaten these pancakes in a
restaurant is with the classic Chinese dish, Peking
Duck. The 'lotus leaf' pancakes are just right for
low-fat dishes, however. Here is one suggestion for a
filling with a Chinese flavour, but any savoury filling
could be used.*

Sieve the flour into a bowl. Boil the water and
the oil and pour into the flour. Stir until blended
and knead well for up to 3 minutes. Divide into 2
pieces and roll each into a sausage shape. Cut
each 'sausage' into 6 pieces (12 pieces in all). Roll
out each piece to a circle 6 inches (15 cm) in
diameter, and sandwich two together. Heat the
frying pan, without fat, to a moderate heat. Put
one 'sandwich' in at a time, and turn it over
when brown spots appear on the underside.
Cook the other side, and peel the pancakes apart
after removing them from the pan. Cover with a
damp tea-towel, while you cook the other
pancakes. Put all the filling ingredients in a pan,
and toss until they are heated through. Divide
them between the pancakes, roll them up and eat
immediately with your fingers.

GRAPEFRUIT AND SEAFOOD STARTER

One serving has 80 kilocalories and 1 g fat
Serves 6

Preparation time 30 minutes + marinating

3 grapefruit
grated rind and juice of 1 lime
4 oz (100 g) shelled prawns
8 oz (225 g) halibut steak, skinned, boned and cut into small pieces
1 tablespoon (15 ml spoon) chopped fresh dill weed or parsley
freshly ground black pepper

Japanese cooking has become very popular, and with it a liking for raw fish. When raw fish is marinated in citrus juice, it appears to cook, because the flesh changes from opaque to white as it does during the cooking process.

Halve the grapefruit, and segment them carefully, removing all the skin with a grapefruit knife as in the first diagram. Cut out the centre pith with scissors as in the second diagram. Put the skinned grapefruit pieces in a bowl. Add the lime juice to the bowl, with the prawns, the fish, the pepper and the fresh herbs. Leave to marinate for at least two hours in a cool place.

To serve, spoon the mixture back into the grapefruit shells, and sprinkle with lime rind.

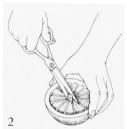

CONSOMMÉ WITH CITRUS ZEST

One serving has 30 kilocalories and negligible fat
Serves 4

Preparation time 15 minutes
Pictured on page 4

1 orange
1 lemon
1 lime
2 × 14½ oz (411 g) can of beef consommé

All the flavour of citrus fruit is in the essential oils of the zest. This soup is easy to prepare and contains a high proportion of Vitamin C.

Peel a little zest from each of the fruits – three pieces from each, measuring approximately 1 inch × ½ inch (2.5 cm × 1.25 cm). Cut them into thin shreds, boil in a little water for 5 minutes to remove the bitterness, and drain. Heat the consommé gently. Squeeze the juice from the fruit and strain it through a fine sieve into the consommé. Heat almost to boiling. Serve in a tureen or individual bowls, garnished with the shreds of zest.

LETTUCE PARCELS

One serving has 160 kilocalories and 2 g fat   Serves 6

Preparation time 15 minutes

12 oz (350 g) minced veal

2 cloves of garlic, crushed

1 tablespoon (15 ml spoon) soy sauce

1 tablespoon (15 ml spoon) red wine vinegar

1 tablespoon (15 ml spoon) dry sherry

1 tablespoon (15 ml spoon) caster sugar

4 oz (100 g) brown rice, cooked

6 well-shaped leaves of iceberg lettuce

These parcels are based on a Malaysian dish. The lettuce leaves should be bowl-shaped as in the diagram, and when the meat has been put in the 'bowl' the leaf is wrapped round the mixture and it is eaten with the hands.

Put the veal in a pan and bring slowly up to heat from cold, stirring all the time. When it has changed colour, drain off any fat and add the other ingredients apart from the lettuce leaves. Stir together for five minutes.

Put one lettuce leaf on each plate. Divide the meat mixture between them and wrap the leaf around the filling.

FISH

White fish such as plaice, cod and haddock contain very low levels of fat, and they are suitable for those on a medically recommended low-fat diet. Oily fish such as herring, mackerel and salmon contain mono-unsaturated and polyunsaturated oils. Shellfish have a cholesterol content, but are very low in fat. There is such a tremendous variety available throughout the year, and there are so many ways of cooking it, without frying in a batter coating, that fish is the ideal low-fat protein food.

Smoked Cod Chowder

Mackerel with Cider Apple Sauce

Whiting with Orange Sauce

25

SMOKED COD CHOWDER

One serving has 115 kilocalories and 1 g fat — Serves 6

Preparation time 20–25 minutes

12 oz (350 g) smoked cod
fillet, skinned

1 medium-size onion,
chopped

1 pint (600 ml) skimmed
milk

1 bay leaf

2 teaspoons (2 × 5 ml
spoon) cornflour

½ pint (300 ml) water

7 oz (198 g) can of
sweetcorn

1 tablespoon (15 ml spoon)
chopped parsley

3 tablespoons (3 × 15 ml
spoon) dry sherry

pepper

*This is a soup which can be a main meal. Serve it with
warm, crusty Granary bread. You can also use borlotti
beans instead of sweetcorn, to make it even more
substantial.*

Poach the fish and chopped onion in the milk for
15 minutes, with a bay leaf for flavouring. Break
up the fish with a fork. Blend the cornflour with
the water and add this to the soup. Bring it to the
boil and simmer until slightly thickened. Add
the sweetcorn and parsley, and re-heat to just
below boiling point. Just before serving add the
sherry and season to taste.

WHITING WITH ORANGE SAUCE

One serving has 200 kilocalories and 2 g fat — Serves 6

Preparation time 20 minutes

6 whiting, filleted and
skinned

2 lbs (900 g) fresh spinach
or 8 oz (250 g) packet of
frozen leaf spinach

½ teaspoon (2.5 ml spoon)
grated nutmeg

2 oranges

1 teaspoon (5 ml spoon)
cornflour

ground white pepper

*Whiting is one of the least expensive fish and is
available for most of the year. It has a well-flavoured,
creamy flesh which blends well with other strong
flavours.*

Season the whiting, and steam them with a little
water on a plate over a pan of boiling water, (or
cook by microwave). Cook the spinach, drain it
very well, and chop it roughly, adding the
nutmeg. Keep it warm while you make the
sauce.

Grate the rind from one of the oranges and
squeeze the juice from both. Blend the rind and

juice with the cornflour in a small pan, adding any liquid from the fish. Bring to the boil, stirring all the time. Arrange the spinach on a warmed serving plate, and lay the fillets on top. Pour over the orange sauce, and serve.

MACKEREL WITH CIDER APPLE SAUCE

One serving has 315 kilocalories and 20 g fat   Serves 4

Preparation time 30 minutes

4 small mackerel, gutted

2 cooking apples

3 tablespoons (3 × 15 ml spoon) dry cider

1 teaspoon (5 ml spoon) powdered ginger

To garnish:

1 tablespoon (15 ml spoon) chopped parsley

slices of lemon

Mackerel, with its distinctive black and silver markings and slightly oily flesh, is best when simply grilled. Gooseberry sauce is often served with mackerel, but this cider apple sauce can be made all the year round. Serve the fish with small potatoes, boiled in their skins, and peas.

Make three diagonal cuts on each side of the mackerel, and put under a hot grill for 5 minutes each side. Keep them warm while you make the sauce.

Peel, core and slice the apples, and stew them in a covered pan with the cider and ginger. When soft, beat them to a pulp, adding more cider, if necessary, to make a pouring consistency. Put the mackerel on a warm serving plate and garnish them with chopped parsley and lemon slices. Serve the apple sauce separately.

MONKFISH STIR-FRY

One serving has 195 kilocalories and 9 g fat

Serves 4

Preparation time 10 minutes + marinating

1 lb (450 g) monkfish

juice of 1 lemon

1 tablespoon (15 ml spoon) chopped parsley

2 tablespoons (2 × 15 ml spoon) sunflower oil

1 medium-size onion, peeled and chopped

4 tomatoes, skinned, de-seeded and chopped

4 oz (100 g) mangetout peas, topped and tailed

2 sticks of celery, sliced

To garnish:

slices of lemon or spring onion flowers

Monkfish has a very firm texture which does not deteriorate on cooking. There are very good frozen mangetout peas available which you can use if the fresh ones are not in season.

Remove any skin or bone from the fish and cut the flesh into strips. Marinate the fish in the lemon juice and the parsley for at least an hour.

Heat the oil in a wok or large frying pan, and stir-fry the chopped onion and fish for 2 minutes. Add the tomatoes, peas and celery and stir-fry for a further 2 minutes. Transfer to a warmed serving plate, and garnish with lemon slices or spring onion flowers.

Chinese-style Baked Salmon Trout

Monkfish Stir-fry

29

CHINESE-STYLE BAKED SALMON TROUT

One serving has 160 kilocalories and 3 g fat   Serves 6

Preparation time 10 minutes + 20–35 minutes cooking

*1 salmon trout weighing
approximately 2 lb (900 g)*

*1 large clove of garlic,
crushed*

*1-inch (2.5 cm) piece of root
ginger, peeled and chopped
finely*

6 spring onions, shredded

*1 tablespoon (15 ml spoon)
sunflower oil*

For the sauce:

*1 teaspoon (5 ml spoon)
cornflour*

*3 tablespoons (3 × 15 ml
spoon) dry sherry*

*2 tablespoons (2 × 15 ml
spoon) soy sauce*

*3 tablespoons (3 × 15 ml
spoon) water*

*1 tablespoon (15 ml spoon)
white wine vinegar*

a few drops of Tabasco sauce

To garnish:

coriander leaves (optional)

Oven temperature:
Gas Mark 4/350°F/180°C

*A whole fish served on a large platter makes a
stunning main course for any party. If you have a fish
kettle, or a large bamboo or metal steamer like the one
illustrated, this dish can be steamed instead of baked
which will give the fish a superior texture. Rainbow
trout (one per person), or for a special occasion a small
sea bass, (when in season, in the summer) are suitable
alternative fish for this dish.*

Preheat the oven. Clean and scale the fish, or
have this done for you at the fish counter. Mix
the garlic, ginger and spring onions, and stuff
the body cavity. Wrap the fish in oiled double
foil and seal it carefully. Bake for 25–35 minutes,
or steam, without foil, for 20 minutes.

Blend all the sauce ingredients together in a
small pan and slowly bring them to the boil,
stirring continuously. Put the fish on a warmed
serving plate, pour over the sauce and garnish it
with coriander leaves, if you like.

BAKED TROUT WITH LIME AND FENNEL

One serving has 210 kilocalories and 7 g fat   Serves 6

Preparation time 10 minutes + 20 minutes baking

6 rainbow trout, gutted

1 bulb of fennel

grated rind and juice of
1 lime

To garnish:

slices of lime

fennel leaves

Oven temperature:
Gas Mark 4/350°F/180°C

Trout have such a lovely flavour and such an attractive appearance that they should be cooked very simply, either by grilling or baking. If you do not like the aniseed flavour of fennel in this recipe, you could just grill the trout with the lime mixture.

Preheat the oven. Wash the trout under cold water and dry them with kitchen paper towelling. Remove any ferny leaves from the fennel and keep them on one side. Slice across the bulb thinly, as in the diagram below. Mix the grated lime rind and juice together. Put a layer of fennel slices in the bottom of an ovenproof dish and lay the trout on top. Brush each fish with the rind and juice mixture, and pour the rest over the top. Cover the dish and bake for 20 minutes. Garnish with the lime slices and fennel leaves.

BISMARCK HERRINGS WITH BEETROOT SAUCE

One serving has 270 kilocalories and 20 g fat   Serves 6

Preparation time 15 minutes + 2 days marinating

6 herrings, filleted

1 onion, peeled and sliced finely

12 white peppercorns

¼ pint (150 ml) spiced vinegar

For the sauce:

2 cooked beetroot, skinned

5.29 oz (150 g) carton of natural yogurt

1 tablespoon (15 ml spoon) horseradish sauce

To garnish:

2 spring onions, sliced

If you are making your own Bismarck herring, you do need to start preparation for this dish two days in advance. You could, of course, cheat, and buy either Bismarck or rollmop herrings in jars or from the delicatessen counter, in which case this dish would take about 10 minutes to prepare at the most.

Lay the herring fillets in a shallow dish, skin side down, and cover them with sliced onion. Sprinkle on the peppercorns, and pour the vinegar over the dish. Cover the dish, and refrigerate for 2 days.

Drain the herring and arrange them on a serving plate. Grate the beetroot and mix it with the yogurt and horseradish sauce. Garnish the herring with spring onions, and serve the sauce separately.

Bismarck Herrings with Beetroot Sauce

ROLLED PLAICE IN RED WINE SAUCE

One serving has 205 kilocalories and 6 g fat   Serves 6

Preparation time 15 minutes + 15 minutes cooking

6 fillets of plaice or sole, skinned

1 tablespoon (15 ml spoon) sunflower oil

1 onion, peeled and chopped

1 carrot, peeled and grated

1 clove of garlic, crushed

¼ pint (150 ml) dry red wine

1 bay leaf

2 oz (50 g) raisins

ground white pepper

To garnish:

1 tablespoon (15 ml spoon) chopped parsley

It is usual to serve white wine with fish, but I have found that this sauce with its strong flavour of raisins is best made with a red wine. The wine colours the fish prettily as well as improving its flavour.

Season the fillets and roll them up, skinned side outside. Heat the oil in a flameproof casserole or a frying pan with a lid. Add the vegetables and garlic, and soften for about 5 minutes. Arrange the fish rolls on the vegetables, add the red wine and a bay leaf and enough water to come half-way up the fish. Simmer the dish for 15 minutes. Plump the raisins by covering them with hot water. Remove the fish to a warmed serving plate. Boil the sauce rapidly until it reduces by half. Drain the raisins and add them to the sauce. Pour over the fish and sprinkle the fillets with chopped parsley.

SMOKED HADDOCK PIE

One serving has 215 kilocalories and 2 g fat   Serves 4

Preparation time 25 minutes   Pictured on page 4
+ 20–30 minutes baking

1 lb (450 g) smoked haddock

½ pint (300 ml) skimmed milk

1½ lb (675 g) potatoes

5.29 oz (150 g) carton of natural yogurt

1 tablespoon (15 ml spoon) cornflour

2 leeks, washed and sliced

ground black pepper

This is a warming, inexpensive winter dish. It can be made up in advance and frozen if you like, and baked just before eating. Serve it with sliced carrots and brussels sprouts.

Poach the haddock in the milk for 5 minutes, and leave for half an hour to infuse. Preheat the oven.

Peel the potatoes, and boil them for approximately 20 minutes. Drain the potatoes when cooked, mash with the yogurt, and season with black pepper. Drain the milk from the fish and blend it with the cornflour in a pan. Bring it to the boil. Remove the skin from the fish and fork the flesh into the sauce. Pour the sauce into the bottom of an ovenproof pie dish. Cover with the sliced leeks, and either pipe the potato on top, or spread it over and smooth the top with a fork. Bake for 20–30 minutes.

PRAWN AND SALMON EN GELÉE

One serving has 125 kilocalories and 6 g fat   Serves 6

Preparation time about 30 minutes + several hours chilling

½ pint (300 ml) water

1.05 oz (30 g) sachet of aspic jelly powder

¼ pint (150 ml) dry white wine

2 oz (50 g) shelled prawns

2 salmon cutlets

3 tomatoes, skinned, de-seeded and chopped

2 tablespoons (2 × 15 ml spoon) chopped chives

To garnish:

shredded lettuce

6 unshelled prawns

This colourful, layered mould cou___ __e served at a summer buffet lunch, or as a start___ __urse. If you cannot find aspic jelly po___ ___achet of gelatine, and make it up with cr___ ___ __ stock.

Heat the water in a pan until just below boiling and s___ __le over the aspic p__ __ __'__. Whisk until t'__ __wder has d___ ved and then stir in the __ __ __e. Put a thin layer in the bottom of a 1¾-pint (1-litre) mould or cake tin. Leave to set for about 30 minutes, and then arrange the shelled prawns on top. Cover with another layer of aspic and leave to set again. Poach the salmon in a very little water for 15 minutes. Leave it to cool completely in the liquid. Skin it and remove the bones, and cut the salmon flesh into cubes. Add to the mould with about half the remaining aspic. Leave the mould to set again. Mix the tomatoes and chives with the remaining aspic and pour into the mould. Chill for about 4 hours until set.

When ready to serve, dip the mould into hot water, and turn it out carefully onto a serving plate. Surround it with shredded lettuce and garnish with unshelled prawns.

MEAT AND POULTRY

It is mistakenly thought that cutting down on meat is the best way of cutting down on fat, but in fact many of the extra lean cuts now sold in Sainsbury's are really well trimmed of fat. Visible fat can also be cut from meat during preparation or on the plate. Poultry generally contains less fat than red meat, and even this can be reduced by removing the skin, where most of the fat is found. Game birds and meat like venison have less fat than farmed animals.

Lamb Fillet with Leek Purée and Rosemary Sauce

Open Sandwich

*Chicken with
Lemon and Artichoke Hearts*

LAMB FILLET WITH LEEK PURÉE AND ROSEMARY SAUCE

One serving has 170 kilocalories and 6 g fat   Serves 6

Preparation time 30–40 minutes + marinating + 15–20 minutes baking

2 teaspoons (2 × 5 ml spoon) chopped rosemary

2 cloves of garlic, crushed

juice of 1 lemon

2 lamb neck fillets

2 lb (900 g) leeks, trimmed, washed and sliced

¼ pint (150 ml) chicken stock

Oven temperature:
Gas Mark 8/450°F/230°C

A pretty dish with the pink lamb slices and the fresh green colour of the purée. Keep the pink and green theme by serving it with green noodles and a radicchio and watercress salad.

Mix 1 teaspoon (5 ml spoon) of the rosemary, the garlic and the lemon juice and brush this over the lamb fillets. Leave to marinate for 2 hours. Preheat the oven. Put lamb and marinade on a shallow baking tray and cover with foil loosely. Roast for no more than 15–20 minutes.

Cook the leeks in 2 tablespoons (2 × 15 ml spoon) chicken stock for 10 minutes. Drain them and reserve the liquid. Purée the leeks in a blender or food processor, and pile onto a warmed serving dish.

Drain any liquid from the lamb, and put this in a small pan with the leek stock, and the remaining chicken stock and rosemary. Boil rapidly until reduced by half.

Slice the lamb thinly and arrange around the purée. Pour the sauce over the lamb slices.

OPEN SANDWICHES

One serving has 385 kilocalories and 10 g fat — Serves 6

Preparation time 15 minutes

6 slices of rye bread

6 lettuce leaves

6 slices of roast topside, trimmed of fat

1 lb (450 g) cottage cheese

1 Granny Smith apple, quartered, cored and sliced

1 orange, sliced across

To garnish:

12 black olives

Though not a main course dish, these open sandwiches provide a substantial and healthy lunch, particularly in the summer. The beef is moister if it has been cooked rare.

Top each piece of bread with a lettuce leaf. Fold the beef slices in half and put on one side of each slice. Put a mound of cottage cheese on the other side. Put slices of apple and a twist of orange in the middle, and garnish with olives.

CHICKEN WITH LEMON AND ARTICHOKE HEARTS

One serving has 220 kilocalories and 8 g fat — Serves 6

Preparation time 10 minutes + 30–40 minutes cooking

6 chicken joints, skinned

1 onion, peeled and chopped

1 tablespoon (15 ml spoon) sunflower oil

thinly grated rind of 1 and juice of 2 lemons

8 oz (228 g) can of butter beans

14 oz (397 g) can of artichoke hearts, drained

1 tablespoon (15 ml spoon) chopped parsley

Chicken has always been looked on as a low-fat meat, and when it has been skinned, even more of the fat disappears. With the lemon and artichokes this is a casserole for summer-time eating. The butter beans thicken the sauce and add fibre.

Flash the chicken joints under a hot grill until sealed on both sides. Soften the onion in the oil in a flameproof casserole, and add the chicken joints. Add the lemon rind and juice to the casserole with the butter beans and the liquid from the can. Cover, and simmer for 20–30 minutes turning occasionally. Add the artichokes and cook for another 10 minutes. Sprinkle with parsley and serve.

SPICED CHICKEN LIVER SHASHLIK

One serving has 205 kilocalories and 8 g fat   Serves 4

Preparation time 20 minutes + marinating

2 × 8 oz (225 g) carton of chicken livers

5.29 oz (150 g) carton of natural yogurt

2 cloves of garlic, peeled

1-inch (2.5 cm) piece of root ginger, peeled

2 teaspoons (2 × 5 ml spoon) paprika pepper

1 teaspoon (5 ml spoon) ground cumin

2 tomatoes, quartered

2 medium-size onions, peeled and quartered

1 green pepper, de-seeded and quartered

1 red pepper, de-seeded and quartered

juice of 1 lemon

The spicy marinade makes all the difference to the chicken livers. It is not used in this case to tenderise the meat, but to add flavour to it. Serve with rice, and a lettuce and cucumber salad.

Rinse the livers in cold water and remove any threads or pieces of fat. Blend the yogurt, garlic, ginger and spices in a liquidiser or food processor. Marinate the livers in this mixture for 2 hours. Thread onto four or eight skewers with the pieces of vegetable. Squeeze over the lemon juice and any remaining marinade and put under a hot grill for 5–10 minutes, turning frequently.

Spiced Chicken Liver Shashlik

CASTEROLED PHEASANT WITH ORANGE RICE

One serving has 555 kilocalories and 14 g fat   Serves 4

Preparation time 20 minutes + 1 hour 15 minutes cooking

*1 plump pheasant,
weighing approx. 2 lb
(900 g)*

8 oz (225 g) brown rice

*1 tablespoon (15 ml spoon)
sunflower oil*

1 onion, peeled and chopped

*grated rind and juice of
1 orange*

*1–1½ pints (600–900 ml)
light stock*

2 oz (50 g) sultanas

1 oz (25 g) cashew nuts

*1 tablespoon (15 ml spoon)
chopped parsley*

To garnish:

orange wedges or slices

Oven temperature:
Gas Mark 2/300°F/150°C

*Although game birds are only in season for part of the
year it is worth taking advantage of them when they
are around, as they do not contain much fat. Young
birds can be plainly roasted, but all birds will be
delicious cooked in a casserole.*

Preheat the oven. Cut pheasant into four joints
as in diagrams 1–3. Rinse the rice under cold
water. Heat the oil in a flameproof casserole and
fry the onion gently until soft. Add the pheasant
joints and fry for 1 minute on each side. Add the
rice and the grated orange rind and juice. Pour
on 1 pint (600 ml) of the stock, cover the
casserole tightly, and cook in the oven for
1 hour.

Plump the sultanas in hot water. Drain, and
add them, the nuts and chopped parsley to the
casserole, pour in more stock if needed, and
return to the oven for another 15 minutes. Serve
garnished with the orange wedges or slices.

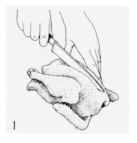

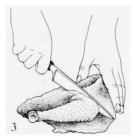

TERIYAKI BEEF OLIVES

One serving has 260 kilocalories and 7 g fat   Serves 4

Preparation time 30 minutes + marinating + 1 hour baking

1 pack of beef for beef olives (4–6 pieces)

1 clove of garlic, peeled and crushed

1-inch (2.5 cm) piece of root ginger, peeled and finely chopped

6 tablespoons (6 × 15 ml spoon) dry sherry

2 tablespoons (2 × 15 ml spoon) soy sauce

1 tablespoon (15 ml spoon) caster sugar

2 large carrots, peeled

4 oz (100 g) french beans

a bunch of spring onions

8 oz (225 g) frozen spinach, thawed, drained and chopped

¼ pint (150 ml) beef stock

2 teaspoons (2 × 5 ml spoon) cornflour

Oven temperature:
Gas Mark 5/375°F/190°C

When sliced, these olives look most attractive, with a whirl of dark green, orange and bright green. The marinade and the sauce add an eastern flavour to what is generally thought of as a British dish. If the special packs of beef for beef olives are not available, use slices of beef topside. Serve this dish with brown rice and more french beans.

Open out the slices of beef, and put them in a large bowl or dish. Blend the garlic and ginger with 1 tablespoon (15 ml spoon) of the sherry and 1 tablespoon (15 ml spoon) of the soy sauce and the sugar, and pour this over the beef. Leave it to marinade for at least one hour. Preheat the oven. Cut the carrots into thin strips about the same size as the beans. Top and tail the beans, and par-boil both carrots and beans for 4 minutes. Trim the spring onions, and split them lengthways. Put the slices on a board and spread them with the spinach. Divide the carrots, beans and onions between the slices. Roll up tightly from the short end, and secure the rolls with fine string or cocktail sticks if necessary. Put them in an ovenproof dish, and brush them with the rest of the marinade. Cover loosely and bake for 1 hour. Remove the string or sticks, and keep the rolls on a warmed serving plate.

Add the stock to the cooking dish and stir in the remaining sherry and soy sauce. Blend the cornflour with a little cold water and stir into the sauce. Boil until thickened and then pour the sauce over the beef olives.

KIDNEYS IN SWEET AND SOUR SAUCE

One serving has 215 kilocalories and 9 g fat

Serves 4

Preparation time 30–45 minutes

6–8 lamb's kidneys, cored and sliced

1 egg white, slightly beaten

1 tablespoon (15 ml spoon) cornflour

2 tablespoons (2 × 15 ml spoon) corn oil

For the sauce:

1-inch (2.5 cm) piece of root ginger, peeled and chopped finely

2 spring onions, chopped finely

1 tablespoon (15 ml spoon) caster sugar

1 teaspoon (5 ml spoon) cornflour

1 tablespoon (15 ml spoon) white wine vinegar

2 tablespoons (2 × 15 ml spoon) dry sherry

1 tablespoon (15 ml spoon) soy sauce

The sauce served with the kidneys is a far cry from the gooey red liquid too often served at Chinese take-away restaurants! You will be amazed how quickly this dish is cooked, once all the ingredients are prepared.

Coat the kidney slices with the egg white. Sprinkle on the cornflour, and turn until they are evenly coated (or shake the slices with the flour in a paper bag until coated). Heat the oil till fairly hot, in a large frying pan or wok and fry the kidneys until they are crisp on the outside, about 4 minutes. Remove them with a slotted spoon, and keep them warm. Add the ginger and spring onions to the pan and stir well. Replace the kidneys and add the sugar. Blend the cornflour with the vinegar, sherry and soy sauce. Add to the pan and stir until the sauce has thickened. Serve immediately.

Kidneys in Sweet and Sour Sauce

Chinese Pork

CHINESE PORK

One serving has 230 kilocalories and 8 g fat   Serves 4

Preparation time 20–30 minutes

1 pork fillet, weighing
approximately 1 lb (450 g)

1 onion, peeled and
quartered

2 teaspoons (2 × 5 ml
spoon) sunflower oil

8 oz (225 g) fresh or frozen
mangetout peas

1-inch (2.5 cm) piece of root
ginger, peeled and chopped
finely

2 cloves of garlic, crushed

1 tablespoon (15 ml spoon)
soy sauce

1 tablespoon (15 ml spoon)
dry sherry

¼ pint (150 ml) beef stock

2 teaspoons (2 × 5 ml
spoon) cornflour

2 spring onions, trimmed
and sliced

Most people think that pork is a fatty meat, but this particular cut, pork fillet, is almost fat-free. All pork can be trimmed well to remove much of the fat. To keep pork really succulent, do not overcook it. The old wives' tale of only eating pork when there is an 'R' in the month dates from a time before refrigeration was common. Pork is available all the year round and keeps for 2–3 days under home refrigeration, loosely covered with foil or clingfilm. In this dish, the thin pork slices are stir-fried until they change colour, leaving them tender and succulent. The vegetables should still be crisp. Serve this with a mixture of green and yellow noodles.

Trim the pork fillet of any visible fat, and cut it across the grain into very thin slices. Separate the 'leaves' of the onion. Heat the oil in a non-stick frying pan and add the onion. Stir-fry for 2–3 minutes. Add the mangetout peas, topped and tailed if fresh, and stir-fry for a further 5 minutes. Remove the onion and peas with a slotted spoon. Add the ginger and garlic to the pan and cook for 1 minute, then increase the heat and add the pork slices. Stir-fry until the meat changes colour then toss in the vegetables. Blend the liquids with the cornflour and add them to the pan, stirring until thickened. Serve sprinkled with the sliced spring onions.

PORK WITH APRICOTS

One serving has 210 kilocalories and 3 g fat   Serves 4

Preparation time 25 minutes + soaking + 1 hour baking

4 oz (100 g) dried apricots

¼ pint (150 ml) orange
juice

A casserole with a creamy flavour and texture, but without the fat or calories of cream. Many kinds of fruit go well with pork, but dried apricots have a high fibre content as a bonus.

Ingredients	
1 lb (450 g) lean pork leg, cubed	Soak the apricots in the orange juice for an hour. Preheat the oven. Trim any visible fat from the pork, and brown it in a non-stick or well-seasoned pan without additional fat. Drain away any fat in the pan, and put the pork in the bottom of a casserole. In the same pan, blend the cornflour and cinnamon with a little water. Add the apricots and juice, bring to the boil and cook until slightly thickened. Pour the sauce over the meat, cover tightly, and cook for 45 minutes in the oven. Stir in the fromage frais and parsley and reheat, but do not allow to boil.
2 teaspoons (2 × 5 ml spoon) cornflour	
1 teaspoon (5 ml spoon) cinnamon	
8 oz (225 g) fromage frais	
1 tablespoon (15 ml spoon) chopped parsley	
Oven temperature: Gas Mark 3/325°F/170°C	

PASTRAMI

One serving has 350 kilocalories and 14 g fat   Serves 6

Preparation time 30 minutes + 4 days marinating + 2½–3 hours cooking

3 lb (1.3 kg) cured silverside

3 cloves of garlic, crushed

1 tablespoon (15 ml spoon) pickling spice

1 teaspoon (5 ml spoon) paprika

½ teaspoon (2.5 ml spoon) cayenne pepper

1 teaspoon (5 ml spoon) ground allspice

2 tablespoons (2 × 15 ml spoon) soft brown sugar

1 medium-size onion, peeled and quartered

6 sprigs of parsley

1 lb (450 g) smoked hock bones, (optional)

Pastrami, beloved of Americans, served hot in rye bread sandwiches, is now available on the delicatessen counter. It is easy to make your own using ready-cured silverside. It is as good served cold in sandwiches, or with a salad, as it is to eat hot. The bacon bones give the pastrami the authentic smoky flavour, but these can be omitted.

Remove the silverside from its wrapper, rinse, and pat it dry. Combine the garlic, the spices and the brown sugar. Rub the surface of the meat with this paste, pressing it in well. Wrap the meat in clingfilm, and put in a covered container in the refrigerator for 4 days, turning it every day.

Unwrap the meat and put it in a large pan, together with any liquid. Just cover with water, and add the remaining ingredients. Bring to simmering point, and simmer for 2½ hours. To eat it hot, leave it in the cooking liquid for 15 minutes, then remove the meat and cut it into very thin slices. To eat it cold, leave it in the cooking liquid until completely cooled, and then slice the meat very thinly.

RABBIT FRICASSEE

One serving has 280 kilocalories and 6 g fat   Serves 4

Preparation time 30 minutes + 1 hour cooking

1 lb (450 g) boneless rabbit, cut into 1-inch (2.5 cm) cubes

2 onions, peeled and quartered

2 carrots, peeled and sliced

2 bay leaves

1 sachet of bouquet garni

1 tablespoon (15 ml spoon) cornflour

½ pint (300 ml) skimmed milk

grated rind and juice of 1 lemon

1 tablespoon (15 ml spoon) chopped parsley

To garnish:

sprigs of watercress

triangles of wholemeal toast

Rabbit is a comparatively low-fat meat, as are most game or wild fowl. Stewing veal makes a good alternative.

Put the rabbit in a pan with the onions, carrots, bay leaves and bouquet garni. Add just enough water to cover the contents. Bring it slowly to the boil and simmer, covered, for 1 hour. Drain the rabbit and vegetables, reserving the stock but discarding the bay leaves and bouquet garni.

Blend the cornflour in the same pan with a little milk. Add the rest of the milk and ¼ pint (150 ml) stock. Bring to the boil, and boil for 2 minutes stirring all the time. Add the grated lemon rind and juice and stir in the meat and vegetables. Heat again but do not boil. Stir in the chopped parsley, transfer to a serving dish, and garnish with watercress and toast triangles.

VEAL MEATBALLS WITH MARSALA AND GRAPE SAUCE

One serving has 255 kilocalories and 7 g fat   Serves 4

Preparation time 15–20 minutes + 15–20 minutes cooking

1 lb (450 g) ground veal

2 oz (50 g) wholemeal breadcrumbs

1 tablespoon (15 ml spoon) chopped parsley

1 tablespoon (15 ml spoon) tomato purée

The flavour of muscatel grapes brings back memories of late summer holidays in Italy, and the Marsala makes the grape flavour even more definite. Sweet sherry or Madeira would make good substitutes. Veal, because it comes from a young animal, contains very little fat. Serve the meatballs with spaghetti or pasta shapes and a lettuce and cucumber salad.

1 small egg (size 5–6), beaten	Mix the veal, breadcrumbs, parsley, tomato purée and egg in a bowl and shape into walnut-sized balls with wetted hands. Heat the oil in a non-stick frying pan and cook the meatballs for about 15 minutes, turning frequently with tongs. Drain off any fat, and add the marsala and grapes. Heat quickly for 5 minutes. Blend the cornflour with a little water and stir into the sauce until thickened.
2 teaspoons (2 × 5 ml spoon) sunflower oil	
¼ pint (150 ml) Marsala	
4 oz (100 g) sweet white grapes, peeled and de-seeded	
1 teaspoon (5 ml spoon) cornflour	

SHARP BEEF STROGANOFF

One serving has 220 kilocalories and 9 g fat   Serves 4

Preparation time 15–20 minutes + 1 hour cooking

3 medium-size onions, peeled and chopped	*Using a non-stick pan, very little additional oil is needed to soften the onions and seal the meat. This dish is usually made with soured cream and brandy, but the substitutes make a perfectly acceptable, low-fat and low-calorie alternative.*
2 teaspoons (2 × 5 ml spoon) sunflower oil	
1 lb (450 g) beef topside or rump steak	
¼ pint (150 ml) beef stock	Put the onions and 1 teaspoon (5 ml spoon) of the oil in a large non-stick pan, and heat slowly until the onions are softened. Remove them with a draining spoon and keep warm. Cut the meat into thin strips and add to the pan with the remaining oil. Fry quickly until sealed. Add the onions, beef stock, Worcestershire sauce and nutmeg and season to taste. Simmer gently, covered, for 45 minutes. Add the mushrooms and simmer for a further 15 minutes. Blend the cornflour with a little water and add it to the pan. Boil until just thickened, remove from the heat and stir in the yogurt. Transfer to a serving dish and sprinkle with paprika pepper.
1 teaspoon (5 ml spoon) Worcestershire sauce	
½ teaspoon (2.5 ml spoon) ground nutmeg	
4 oz (100 g) mushrooms, sliced	
1 tablespoon (15 ml spoon) cornflour	
5.29 oz (150 g) carton of natural yogurt	
paprika pepper	
freshly ground black pepper	

BEEF WITH BLACKBERRIES

One serving has 300 kilocalories and 11 g fat — Serves 6

Preparation time 15 minutes + 30–45 minutes baking

2 lb (900 g) fillet of beef

1 tablespoon (15 ml spoon) corn oil

¼ pint (150 ml) beef stock

4 tablespoons (4 × 15 ml spoon) port

2 teaspoons (2 × 5 ml spoon) cornflour

4–6 oz (100–175 g) fresh or frozen blackberries, or 7½ oz (213 g) can of blackberries in natural juice, drained

ground black pepper

Oven temperature:
Gas Mark 8/450°F/230°C

Often the combination of fruit with meat does not raise an eyebrow: think, for instance, of roast pork and apple sauce, duck with orange, or turkey with cranberries. When more unusual combinations are made, however, they are often tried with some trepidation. This dish has nevertheless proved a favourite, and although best with fresh blackberries, it can also be made with frozen ones, or those canned in natural juice. Serve with a green vegetable, such as french beans or mangetout peas.

Preheat the oven. Trim any fat or silvery 'skin' from the beef. Brush with the oil, season with pepper and roast in the oven for 30–45 minutes (rare to medium rare). Remove the meat, wrap it in foil and keep it warm. Drain any fat from the roasting tin and add the beef stock. Stir well, scraping all the meaty pieces from the base of the pan. Blend the port with the cornflour, add this to the pan and stir until thickened. Stir in the blackberries. Season to taste. Cut the meat into thick slices and arrange it on a plate. Pour the sauce over it.

CALF'S LIVER WITH ORANGE

One serving has 220 kilocalories and 8 g fat — Serves 4

Preparation time 25–30 minutes

1 lb (450 g) calf's liver, sliced

grated rind and juice of 1 small orange

¼ pint (150 ml) light stock or white wine

freshly ground black pepper

Lamb's liver could also be used for this dish, but the flavour of calf's liver is much more subtle. Whichever you use, cooking must be kept to a minimum, so that the inside is still pink and the liver is moist.

Rinse the liver in cold water, and pat dry with kitchen paper towelling. Sprinkle half of the orange rind onto the liver slices. Press it in and season the slices with pepper. Turn the liver over, and repeat using the rest of the rind. Put the slices on the rack of a grillpan and squeeze the juice of the orange over the liver. Grill under a high heat for about 2 minutes, when the orange juice should have burned a little on the base of the pan. Turn the liver over. Add the stock to the pan, and grill for another 2 minutes. Put the liver on a warmed serving dish. Heat the sauce in the grill pan and pour it over the liver. Garnish with 4 orange wedges and the watercress.

SALAD WITH CALF'S LIVER

One serving has 230 kilocalories and 14 g fat   Serves 6

Preparation time 30 minutes

8 oz (225 g) young spinach leaves

2 large carrots, peeled and sliced

2 tablespoons (2 × 15 ml spoon) sunflower oil

1 medium-size red onion, chopped

1 lb (500 g) calf's liver, cut into thin strips

4 oz (100 g) button mushrooms, thinly sliced

1 oz (25 g) small black olives

2 tablespoons (2 × 15 ml spoon) red wine vinegar

Warm salads, or salades tièdes, need to be served immediately, although the vegetable preparation can be done in advance. A good combination of textures and flavours makes this salad interesting. Serve it with warm wholemeal bread.

Wash the spinach leaves and dry them well. Cut the carrot slices into flower shapes using a small, fluted cutter as in the diagram. Put the spinach and carrots in a salad bowl. Heat the oil in a large pan or wok, and gently fry the chopped onion until translucent. Turn up the heat and add the liver and the mushrooms, and fry until the liver changes colour (about 2 minutes). Remove the onion, liver and mushrooms from the pan with a draining spoon, and add to the bowl, with the olives. Put the vinegar in the pan and heat it rapidly, stirring in all the sediment. Pour over the salad, and toss all the ingredients together.

TURKEY WITH CRANBERRY SAUCE

One serving has 245 kilocalories and 2 g fat   Serves 6

Preparation time 15 minutes + 1 hour 45 minutes baking

2 small oranges

1¾–2 lb (800–900 g)
boneless turkey roast

8 oz (225 g) cranberries

1 teaspoon (15 ml spoon)
ground cinnamon

2 oz (50 g) sugar

oil, for greasing

Oven temperature:
Gas Mark 5/375°F/190°C

Cranberries are a traditional accompaniment for the American Thanksgiving Day turkey. This treatment of the two main ingredients give a new look to the traditional dish. Serve it with small potatoes boiled in their skins, and mangetout peas.

Preheat the oven. Peel one orange, remove the pith and cut into thin slices. Arrange the slices on the roast. Wrap the meat in oiled greaseproof paper and bake for 1¾ hours. Grate the rind and squeeze the juice of the second orange, and simmer them in a pan, with the cranberries and cinnamon, until the cranberry skins pop. Add the sugar and stir until dissolved. Sieve the sauce and keep it warm. When the turkey is cooked, remove the string and slice it thickly. Arrange the meat slices on a warmed plate. Pour over some of the sauce as a garnish and serve the rest separately.

Turkey with Cranberry Sauce

CHICKEN AND MANGO EN PAPILLOTE

One serving has 225 kilocalories and 5 g fat   Serves 6

Preparation time 10 minutes + 30 minutes baking

1 ripe mango

1 tablespoon (15 ml spoon) chopped chives

8 oz (227 g) carton of skimmed milk soft cheese

6 skinless, boneless chicken breasts

juice of 1 lemon

oil, for greasing (if necessary)

Oven temperature:
Gas Mark 5/375°F/190°C

These little parcels should be served in their own wrapping. The aroma when they are opened is delicious, and there is also the surprise of finding out what is inside. Make sure the paper or foil is well sealed, as part of the cooking is done by the steam inside. Serve with potatoes boiled in their skins and a slightly bitter chicory salad, to offset the sweetness of the mango.

Preheat the oven. Cut the mango into 3 (diagram 1), peel it, cut up the flesh into small pieces and blend it in a bowl with the chives and soft cheese. Open up the slit in the chicken where the bone has been removed (diagram 2) and spoon in the mango mixture. Sprinkle the chicken pieces with the lemon juice.

Make a parcel of each breast, either in oiled foil or greaseproof paper, sealing well, and bake for 30 minutes.

VENISON CHOPS WITH PARSNIP SAUCE

One serving has 470 kilocalories and 15 g fat   Serves 4

Preparation time 35 minutes

½ pint (300 ml) skimmed milk

2 medium-size parsnips, peeled and cubed

1 medium-size potato, peeled and cubed

1 tablespoon (15 ml spoon) Dijon mustard

4 venison chops

1 tablespoon (15 ml spoon) sunflower oil

2 teaspoons (2 × 5 ml spoon) Meaux mustard

To garnish:

sprigs of watercress

Venison contains very little fat. It has a more 'gamey' flavour than beef, but can be cooked in the same way. It should not be overcooked, because it has a tendency to become dry. This dish is excellent served with small potatoes boiled in their skins, and a green vegetable.

Heat the skimmed milk with the parsnips and potatoes, and simmer until tender. Stir in the Dijon mustard. Liquidise or process and keep warm. Brush the chops with oil and grill for 5 minutes on each side. Keep on a warmed serving dish. Stir the Meaux mustard and any juices from the meat into the sauce. Garnish the chops with watercress and serve with the sauce.

VEAL ESCALOPES WITH VERMOUTH

One serving has 250 kilocalories and 5 g fat   Serves 4

Preparation time 20 minutes + marinating

4 veal escalopes

¼ pint (150 ml) dry vermouth

1 onion, peeled and chopped

1 tablespoon (15 ml spoon) green peppercorns

2 tablespoons (2 × 15 ml spoon) peach chutney

To garnish:

sprigs of watercress

The aromatic flavour of vermouth makes a good base for a sauce. The peach chutney adds a fruity sharpness. Serve with potatoes boiled in their skins, and leaf spinach.

Marinate the escalopes in the vermouth, onion and peppercorns for at least one hour. Remove from the marinade and put them under a hot grill for about 3 minutes each side, depending on their size and thickness. Add the chutney to the marinade in a small pan and boil it rapidly until it is reduced by half. Put the escalopes on a warmed serving dish, and pour the sauce over them. Garnish with watercress.

PASTA AND RICE

Both these ingredients can be the basis of interesting low-fat dishes because they contain no intrinsic fat (apart from the little in egg noodles). Brown rice, containing the husk, and wholemeal pasta are also very high in fibre.

Lamb Biryani

Sea Shell Salad

Noodles with
Fromage Frais

LAMB BIRYANI

One serving has 330 kilocalories and 11 g fat   Serves 6

Preparation time 20 minutes + marinating + 1 hour baking

2 tablespoons (2 × 15 ml spoon) corn oil

1 onion, chopped finely

1 clove of garlic, peeled and crushed

2 teaspoons (2 × 5 ml spoon) ground cardamom

1-inch (2.5 cm) piece of root ginger, peeled and chopped

6–12 cloves, to taste

1 teaspoon (5 ml spoon) chilli powder

2 teaspoons (2 × 5 ml spoon) ground coriander

2 teaspoons (2 × 5 ml spoon) ground cumin

1 teaspoon (5 ml spoon) turmeric

1 lb (450 g) lean lamb, cubed

5.29 oz (150 g) carton of natural yogurt

8 oz (225 g) basmati rice

2 bay leaves

2 green chillis, de-seeded and chopped finely

3 tablespoons (3 × 15 ml spoon) lemon juice

To garnish:

1 small onion, peeled and sliced

a few coriander leaves

Oven temperature:
Gas Mark 3/325°F/170°C

This is the spicy brother of Vegetable Pilau (page 66). The addition of green chillis and chilli powder give it a powerful flavour. Serve it with a cooling dish like cucumber raita (cubed cucumber in natural yogurt). The ingredients list may look formidable, but when all the spices have been amassed, it is a simple dish to make.

Heat the oil in a flameproof casserole, and soften the onion and garlic in it. Add all the spices, the lamb and the yogurt and stir until the meat changes colour. Remove from the heat, cover, and leave to marinate for at least half an hour and preferably overnight.

Rinse the rice and cook it with the bay leaves in plenty of boiling water for 5–6 minutes, then drain and pour into the casserole. Sprinkle with chillis and pour over the lemon juice. Cover tightly, and bake for 1 hour. Before serving, stir well to combine the lamb and rice. Divide the sliced onions into rings and arrange on the rice with the coriander leaves.

SEA SHELL SALAD

One serving has 255 kilocalories and 3 g fat — Serves 6

Preparation time 10–15 minutes

8 oz (225 g) pasta shells

8 oz (225 g) shelled prawns

6 tablespoons (6 × 15 ml spoon) low-calorie oil and vinegar dressing

3 tablespoons (3 × 15 ml spoon) chopped parsley

To garnish:

1 lemon, cut in 6 wedges

6 unshelled prawns

This mixture of shellfish and pasta is always a popular starter or dish for a buffet party. I like this combination of pink and green, but you may prefer to experiment with other types of pasta and fish.

Cook the pasta shells in plenty of boiling water for 8 minutes. Drain, and toss them together with the shelled prawns, dressing and parsley. Garnish with lemon wedges and unshelled prawns.

NOODLES WITH FROMAGE FRAIS

One serving has 125 kilocalories and less than 1 g fat — Serves 6

Preparation time 10 minutes

8 oz (225 g) fresh green noodles

half a 1 lb (500 g) carton of fromage frais

1 tablespoon (15 ml spoon) chopped fresh basil or parsley

2 cloves of garlic, crushed

freshly ground black pepper

This is the nearest low-fat equivalent to pasta with pesto. It is so simple to make that a meal could be ready in under 15 minutes. Serve it with a salad, followed by fresh fruit. Dried pasta can, of course, be used instead of fresh noodles.

Cook the noodles in plenty of boiling water for 2 minutes or according to manufacturers' instructions, and drain them. Mix the other ingredients together, and toss in the pasta. Mix well again and serve immediately.

JEWELLED PASTA

One serving has 130 kilocalories and 3 g fat   Serves 6

Preparation time 12 minutes

8.82 oz (250 g) packet of
pasta twists

8 oz (225 g) broccoli

1 red pepper, de-seeded

1 tablespoon (15 ml spoon)
sunflower oil

*The broccoli and pepper retain both their colour and
crisp texture when given just a brief blanching. This
dish would go well with a meaty casserole, or a fish
dish with sauce. As a supper dish on its own, it should
be sprinkled liberally with grated low-fat hard cheese.*

Boil the pasta in a large pan for 8 minutes. Divide
the broccoli into tiny florets and cut the pepper
up into ½-inch (1 cm) squares. Put the two in a
basin. Drain the water from the pasta over the
vegetables and leave them for 2 minutes. Drain
the vegetables. Toss the pasta and vegetables
with the oil.

CANNELLONI

One serving has 230 kilocalories and 2 g fat   Serves 6

Preparation time 15–20 minutes + 25–30 minutes baking

8 oz (225 g) mushrooms

2 medium-size onions

1 clove of garlic

4 oz (100 g) lean cooked
ham

18 cannelloni tubes

14 oz (397 g) can of
chopped tomatoes with
herbs, or 14 oz (397 g) can
of chopped tomatoes and
1 teaspoon (5 ml spoon)
mixed herbs

1 tablespoon (15 ml spoon)
tomato purée

oil, for greasing

Oven temperature:
Gas Mark 6/400°F/200°C

*Serve this Italian dish with either braised fennel or a
fennel and tomato salad. The attractive fennel leaves
can then be used as a garnish for the cannelloni dish.*

Wipe the mushrooms, peel one of the onions and
the garlic, and liquidise, process or mince all
three with the ham. Divide the stuffing between
the cannelloni tubes, and put them in an oiled,
ovenproof dish.
   Peel and chop the other onion finely, and mix
with the chopped tomatoes and purée. Spoon
over the tubes so that they are all coated. Cover
and bake for 25–30 minutes.

*Jewelled Pasta
Cannelloni*

CHICKEN AND MACARONI CASSEROLE

One serving has 295 kilocalories and 5 g fat   Serves 6

Preparation time 20 minutes + 1 hour baking

6 chicken thighs
2 oz (50 g) lean ham, chopped
1 onion, peeled and chopped finely
2 cloves of garlic, crushed
6 courgettes sliced
14 oz (397 g) can of chopped tomatoes
2 teaspoons (2 × 5 ml spoon) mixed herbs
8 oz (225 g) macaroni
½ pint (300 ml) chicken stock

Oven temperature:
Gas Mark 3/325°F/170°C

A very useful and economical dish. Leftover cooked meat can be used instead of chicken, and the vegetables can be varied according to what you have available. Serve it with a crisp green salad.

Fry the chicken thighs in a non-stick pan without fat. Remove from the pan and add the ham, onion and garlic. Stir over a low heat until the onion is soft. Remove the skin from the chicken. Put the onion mixture and skinned chicken in a casserole. Add the courgettes, tomatoes, herbs and macaroni and enough stock to cover. Cover the casserole and bake for 1 hour.

RICE-STUFFED CABBAGE

One serving has 135 kilocalories and less than 1 g fat   Serves 6

Preparation time 30 minutes + 1 hour baking

1 medium-size onion, peeled and chopped finely
2 cloves of garlic, crushed
6 oz (175 g) easy-cook American rice
1 tablespoon (15 ml spoon) tomato purée
1 tablespoon (15 ml spoon) chopped parsley
½ pint (300 ml) chicken stock
12 large cabbage leaves

Even people who do not normally like cabbage seem to enjoy this dish. The same stuffing could also be used for vine leaves.

Mix together the onion, garlic, rice, tomato purée, parsley, pepper and enough stock to make a stiff mixture. Blanch the cabbage leaves in a large pan of boiling water for 2–4 minutes, depending on thickness. Rinse them in cold water and then spread them out on a work surface. Trim away the coarse centre stem, as shown in the diagram, and divide the stuffing between each leaf. Wrap the stuffing up in the leaf to form loose parcels. Put the remaining

14 oz (397 g) can of
chopped tomatoes with
herbs, or 14 oz (397 g) can
of chopped tomatoes and
1 teaspoon (5 ml spoon)
mixed herbs

freshly ground black pepper

Oven temperature:
Gas Mark 3/325°F/170°C

stock and the canned tomatoes in the bottom of
an ovenproof casserole and arrange the cabbage
parcels on top. Cover the dish tightly and bake
for 1 hour.

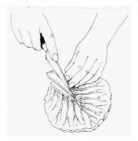

PRAWN JAMBALAYA

One serving has 455 kilocalories and 10 g fat   Serves 4

Preparation time 10 minutes + 35 minutes cooking

2 tablespoons (2 × 15 ml
spoon) sunflower oil

2 cloves of garlic, crushed

1 medium-size onion,
peeled and chopped

1 green pepper, de-seeded
and chopped roughly

4 oz (100 g) lean ham, diced

8 oz (225 g) shelled prawns

8 oz (225 g) Italian rice

2 × 14 oz (397 g) can
chopped tomatoes with
herbs, or 2 × 14 oz (397 g)
can chopped tomatoes and 2
teaspoons (2 × 5 ml spoon)
mixed herbs

¼ pint (150 ml) dry white
wine

*A jambalaya is a peasant rice dish which originated in
Louisiana, in the deep South of the United States.
Ham and prawns are the two basic ingredients, but
other meats, for example, chicken, could be added. It is
a marvellous party dish, which can be stretched to be
more economical with the addition of more rice.*

Heat the oil in a flameproof casserole and gently
fry the garlic, onion and pepper until softened.
Add the ham and prawns and fry for a further
two minutes. Rinse the rice in cold water and
add to the casserole with the tomatoes, herbs (if
used) and wine. Bring to the boil, cover, and
simmer for 35 minutes.

RICE AND TOMATO SOUP

One serving has 90 kilocalories and less than 1 g fat   Serves 6

Preparation time 15 minutes + 30 minutes cooking

1 large onion, peeled and chopped finely

14 oz (397 g) can of chopped tomatoes

1 tablespoon (15 ml spoon) tomato purée

2 oz (50 g) long grain rice

1½ pints (900 ml) well-flavoured chicken stock

1 oz (25 g) plain flour

½ pint (300 ml) skimmed milk

freshly ground black pepper

This soup has a much better flavour if it can be made with stock from a chicken carcass, rather than from stock cubes, and this will have the additional advantage of adding less salt to the dish. The canned tomatoes may be replaced by 8 oz (225 g) fresh tomatoes, skinned and chopped.

Put the onion, tomatoes and tomato purée, rice and chicken stock in a pan, and bring it to the boil. Then cover the pan, and simmer for 30 minutes. Whisk the flour and milk together until smooth. Add this to the soup, season, and bring to the boil again until thickened.

Rice and Tomato Soup

Vegetable Pilau

Kedgeree

VEGETABLE PILAU

One serving has 165 kilocalories and 3 g fat   Serves 6

Preparation time 25 minutes

1 onion, peeled and chopped finely
1 clove of garlic, crushed
1 tablespoon (15 ml spoon) corn oil
2 teaspoons (2 × 5 ml spoon) ground cardamom
1 teaspoon (5 ml spoon) turmeric
6–12 cloves, to taste
1 teaspoon (5 ml spoon) ground cumin
1 teaspoon (5 ml spoon) ground cinnamon
4 oz (100 g) cauliflower florets
4 oz (100 g) frozen peas
2 oz (50 g) sultanas
6 oz (175 g) basmati rice, rinsed

There are two types of Indian rice dish, the pilau and the biryani (page 58). The pilau does not contain hot spices, and can therefore be served with any other meat or vegetable dish without overpowering the other flavours.

In a fairly large pan, soften the onion and garlic in the oil, then add the spices and fry for 1 minute. Break up the cauliflower into tiny pieces, and add with the peas and sultanas to the pan. Stir for half a minute, then add the rice and ½ pint (300 ml) water. Bring to the boil, stirring occasionally. Cover tightly and simmer for 15 minutes. Stir occasionally and add a little more warm water if necessary. Transfer to a serving bowl.

KEDGEREE

One serving has 280 kilocalories and 11 g fat   Serves 6

Preparation time 10 minutes + 15–20 minutes cooking

12 oz (350 g) packet of smoked mackerel fillets
6 oz (175 g) American easy-cook rice, rinsed
1–2 teaspoons (1–2 × 5 ml spoon) mild curry powder
half a green pepper, de-seeded and chopped

Kedgeree with smoked haddock is traditionally a breakfast dish. Not many of us have the time to cook such a dish early in the morning, so I have substituted sweetcorn and green pepper for hard-boiled egg, and I find that this makes a warming supper dish. I used the Cornish Cove Mackerel with a sachet of mustard and whisky which gave the dish even more warmth, but you could stir in 1 tablespoon (15 ml spoon) Meaux-type mustard to give a similar effect.

4 oz (100 g) sweetcorn

5.29 oz (150 g) carton of natural yogurt

To garnish:

wedges of lemon

Put the mackerel fillets in a jug or a shallow dish and cover them with boiling water. Put the rice in a pan, cover with ¾ pint (450 ml) water and add the curry powder. Bring to the boil, and then cover tightly and simmer for 10 minutes. Stir in the pepper and sweetcorn and simmer for a further 10 minutes, when all the water should have been absorbed.

Skin the mackerel, and fork the flesh into the rice. Stir in the yogurt. Turn onto a warmed serving plate and garnish with lemon wedges.

GOLDEN RICE SALAD

One serving has 250 kilocalories and 6 g fat   Serves 6

Preparation time 15 minutes

8 oz (225 g) easy-cook American rice

a few threads of saffron or 1 teaspoon (5 ml spoon) turmeric

2 carrots, peeled and grated

2 oranges, peeled and segmented

5.29 oz (150 g) carton of lemon flavoured yogurt

1 tablespoon (15 ml spoon) lemon juice

2 tablespoons (2 × 15 ml spoon) sunflower oil

ground black pepper

Saffron is an expensive ingredient, but it gives a subtle colouring and flavouring to rice. Use it in this dish if you can. Turmeric is the spice which gives curries their yellow colouring and the whole effect of the salad will be more brilliant than golden, although still very appetising.

Rinse the rice, and put in a pan with ½ pint (300 ml) of water, and the saffron or turmeric. Bring to the boil, cover, and simmer for 12 minutes, or until all the water is absorbed. Turn the rice into a salad bowl, and add all other ingredients. Toss together well, and serve immediately.

VEGETABLES AND SALADS

One of the most usual ways to serve a plainly-cooked vegetable is to toss in a knob of butter. In this book other ways of dressing cooked vegetables have been used to provide flavour and an attractive appearance, without added fat. Béchamel-type sauces can be made by the blended method to coat cooked vegetables, and a tomato and garlic sauce not only adds flavour, but colour as well. Try using less salt or no salt at all when cooking vegetables and cook them for the minimum length of time so that there is still a 'bite' left to the texture. Raw, fresh vegetables contain the maximum amount of nutrients, and have virtually no fat content. They are high in fibre too, and so an obvious, healthy choice for a low-fat cook. You can even use a little oil high in polyunsaturates (such as sunflower or safflower) in the dressing!

Mushroom Salad

Red Salad

French Beans
in Tomato Sauce

69

FRENCH BEANS IN TOMATO SAUCE

One serving has 28 kilocalories and 1 g fat

Serves 6

Preparation time 15–20 minutes

2 teaspoons (2 × 5 ml spoon) corn oil

1 onion, peeled and chopped

2 cloves of garlic, peeled and crushed

7 oz (200 g) can of tomatoes, drained and chopped

1 teaspoon (5 ml spoon) mixed herbs

1 tablespoon (15 ml spoon) tomato purée

12 oz (375 g) french beans, topped and tailed

ground black pepper

A colourful vegetable to serve with any grill or roast. It also goes well with fish dishes.

Heat the oil in a pan gently and soften the onion and garlic. Add the tomatoes, herbs and tomato purée and simmer the sauce for 15 minutes. Rinse the beans and boil them for 4 minutes in water, then drain them well. Season the tomato sauce and toss in the beans. Raise the heat for half a minute and then serve immediately.

MUSHROOM SALAD

One serving has 20 kilocalories and less than 1 g fat

Serves 6

Preparation time 5 minutes + chilling

1 lb (450 g) small mushrooms

1 lemon

4 tablespoons (4 × 15 ml spoon) fromage frais

1 tablespoon (15 ml spoon) chopped parsley

1 tablespoon (15 ml spoon) chopped chives

1 tablespoon (15 ml spoon) chopped capers

This simple, summery salad goes well with a plain grilled steak or with liver. It can also be used as a starter course.

Wipe and slice the mushrooms and put them in a serving bowl. Grate the rind of the lemon finely and squeeze the juice. Mix the rind and juice with the other ingredients. Pour over the mushrooms, mix well and leave in the refrigerator for 1 hour.

RED SALAD

One serving has 50 kilocalories and 2 g fat   Serves 6

Preparation time 20 minutes

---

1 head of radicchio

4 medium-size tomatoes, skinned

1 red onion, peeled

4 oz (100 g) radishes, topped and tailed

half a red pepper, de-seeded

3 tablespoons (3 × 15 ml spoon) tomato juice

1 tablespoon (15 ml spoon) lemon juice

1 teaspoon (5 ml spoon) caster sugar

1 teaspoon (5 ml spoon) sunflower oil

Although radicchio looks like red lettuce, it is a member of the chicory family and has a slightly bitter flavour. It is sometimes known as red chicory. It blends well with other vegetables which are sweeter, such as tomatoes or peppers.

Peel each leaf separately from the radicchio head. Rinse the leaves, dry them, and arrange them on a large platter.

Chop the tomatoes and onion and mix them together. Slice the radishes and cut the pepper into thin strips. Blend the tomato juice and lemon juice with the sugar and oil. Mix this dressing with the chopped and sliced vegetables and spoon into the leaves.

SALAD DRESSINGS

A good dressing can add a whole new dimension to a salad. Most of the traditional dressings are based on oils, but low-fat alternatives can be based on natural yogurt or fruit juices with flavourings such as freshly chopped herbs, different flavours of mustard or spices. Try yogurt with chopped mint with a cucumber and tomato salad, or orange juice and cinnamon with a watercress and nut salad. A mere teaspoonful of oil, either olive or sunflower, will give an added gloss, particularly to green leaf salads, without adding a lot of fat.

SPINACH AND COURGETTE MOUSSE

One serving has 70 kilocalories and 3 g fat

Serves 6

Preparation time 30 minutes + 1 hour baking

1 lb (450 g) fresh young
spinach

½ teaspoon (2.5 ml spoon)
ground nutmeg

1 tablespoon (15 ml spoon)
sunflower oil, plus extra for
greasing

1 onion, peeled and chopped

2 cloves of garlic, peeled and
crushed

1 lb (450 g) courgettes,
sliced

3 egg whites

To garnish:

2 carrots, grated

Oven temperature:
Gas Mark 4/350°F/180°C

*A bold contrast of colours, flavours and texture make
this an attractive dish for a summer lunch party.
Besides being served as a side dish, it could also be used
as a starter course.*

Wash and trim the spinach. Cook, covered, over
a low heat in just the water clinging to the leaves
for 10 minutes. Drain well and liquidise or put
through a food processor, with the nutmeg.
Heat the oil in the same pan and soften the onion
and garlic in it. Add the courgettes and cook,
covered, for 15 minutes. Liquidise or process,
and season. Whisk the egg whites, and fold half
into each purée. Put the spinach purée into an
oiled soufflé dish and carefully spoon the
courgette purée over it. Stand the dish in a
roasting tin, with water half-way up the side of
the dish as in the diagram, and bake for 1 hour or
until firm to touch, in a preheated oven. Loosen
the edges and turn it out carefully onto a warmed
plate. Garnish the mousse with grated carrot.

Spinach and Courgette Mousse

CRACKED WHEAT SALAD

One serving has 90 kilocalories and less than 1 g fat   Serves 6

Preparation time 10 minutes + soaking

4 oz (100 g) cracked wheat

¼ cucumber, thickly sliced and cubed

4 medium-size tomatoes, skinned, de-seeded and chopped

2 sticks of celery, sliced

1 tablespoon (15 ml spoon) chopped chives

2 tablespoons (2 × 15 ml spoon) fromage frais

juice of 1 lemon

ground black pepper

To garnish:

mint leaves

Cracked wheat (or bulghur wheat) is a grain which, when soaked in water, swells to about twice its original size, and then needs no further preparation apart from draining and squeezing out the liquid. It is used as a base for a classical Middle Eastern salad, Tabbouleh, but it combines well with most salad ingredients. Cracked wheat can be bought in health food shops.

Soak the cracked wheat in plenty of cold water for at least 30 minutes. Drain it in a sieve, and press out any excess water. Mix the wheat in a serving bowl with all the other ingredients, season very well, and garnish with the mint leaves.

KOHLRABI AU GRATIN

One serving has 70 kilocalories and 2 g fat   Serves 6

Preparation time 30 minutes

3 kohlrabi, trimmed

1 teaspoon (5 ml spoon) lemon juice

1 rounded tablespoon (2 × 15 ml spoon) cornflour

½ pint (300 ml) skimmed milk

1 tablespoon (15 ml spoon) Dijon mustard

2 oz (50 g) low-fat hard cheese, grated

1 tablespoon (15 ml spoon) wholemeal breadcrumbs

Kohlrabi is not a root vegetable, although it has a flavour quite like a turnip. When sold, most of the outer leaves have been trimmed, otherwise it would resemble a cabbage with a turnip-like stem. It can be eaten hot as in this dish, or grated and used raw in salads.

If the kohlrabi are young there is no need to peel them. Cut them into ½-inch (1 cm) slices and boil in enough water to cover, with the lemon juice, for 15 minutes. Drain the kohlrabi, reserving the vegetable stock. Blend the cornflour with a little milk in the same pan, and then add the remaining milk. Bring it slowly to the boil, stirring all the time. Remove from the heat, and add the mustard, most of the grated cheese, and enough vegetable stock to give the sauce a coating consistency. Add the kohlrabi and toss it in the sauce. Pour into an ovenproof serving dish. Sprinkle with the breadcrumbs and remaining cheese, and grill until the top is crisp and golden.

STUFFED RED PEPPERS

One serving has 180 kilocalories and 5 g fat   Serves 6

Preparation time 15 minutes + 45 minutes baking

3 red peppers

15.5 oz (439 g) can of pease pudding

5.29 oz (150 g) carton of natural yogurt

1 teaspoon (5 ml spoon) turmeric

1 teaspoon (5 ml spoon) Dijon mustard

2 cloves of garlic, peeled

4 oz (100 g) Edam cheese, grated

oil, for greasing

Oven temperature:
Gas Mark 4/350°F/180°C

A dish for a winter's day, or to accompany a casserole. The flame colours make you feel warm even before you start eating!

Cut the peppers in half lengthways and remove the stalks and seeds. Plunge them into boiling water for 5 minutes, drain them and put the shells on an oiled baking sheet or ovenproof dish. Blend the pease pudding, yogurt, turmeric, mustard and garlic in a liquidiser or food processor, and divide the mixture between the pepper shells. Sprinkle them with cheese, and bake, covered with foil, for 45 minutes. Remove the foil for the last 10 minutes to crisp the tops.

POTATO AND ONION SLICE

One serving has 155 kilocalories and 1 g fat   Serves 4

Preparation time 15 minutes + 1 hour 15 minutes baking

1 lb (450 g) medium-size
potatoes, scrubbed

3 medium-size onions,
peeled

¼ pint (150 ml) skimmed
milk

1 teaspoon (5 ml spoon)
dried sage

1 oz (25 g) wholemeal
breadcrumbs

1 oz (25 g) low-calorie hard
cheese, grated

Oven temperature:
Gas Mark 4/350°F/180°C

*If you have the time, baked potato dishes can be
extremely useful. They can be cooked at the same time
as a casserole and the crispy texture of the topping
makes a contrast to the tender ingredients in the
casserole. Different herbs can be used to complement
whatever the dish is accompanying, for example, use
sage to accompany pork or thyme for chicken.*

Cut the potatoes and onions into even, ¼-inch
(5 mm) slices. Arrange in alternate layers in an
oiled ovenproof dish finishing with a layer of
potatoes. Mix the milk with the sage and pour it
into the dish, then combine the breadcrumbs
with the cheese and sprinkle them over the top.
Cover the dish, and bake for 1 hour, and then for
a further 15 minutes uncovered, to crisp the top.

TUNA BAKED POTATOES

One serving has 290 kilocalories and 12 g fat   Serves 6

Preparation time 20 minutes + 1–1¼ hours baking

6 potatoes for baking

8 oz (227 g) carton of
skimmed milk soft cheese

2 × 7 oz (198 g) can of tuna
in brine, drained

2 tablespoons (2 × 15 ml
spoon) capers, chopped

2 oz (50 g) low-fat hard
cheese, grated

Oven temperature:
Gas Mark 6/400°F/200°C

*Now that potatoes are sold specifically for baking, it is
easy to get the right number of a similar size. Use
Maris Pipers or King Edwards if you can't get the
special ones. I find that the crunchy potato skin is just
as delicious as the filling.*

Preheat the oven. Slit the potato skins round the
middle and bake them for about 1¼ hours. If
you push the potatoes onto metal skewers to
bake, it will speed up the cooking process,
saving time and fuel. They are cooked when
they feel soft when squeezed, wrapped in a clean
cloth or kitchen paper towelling to protect the
hand.
    Split them in half when cooked, scoop out the
flesh, and mash together with the soft cheese,

tuna and capers. Pile the stuffing back into the potato skins and sprinkle with grated hard cheese. Put them under a hot grill until the filling is golden brown and bubbling.

STUFFED ONIONS

One serving has 130 kilocalories and 2 g fat	Serves 4

Preparation time 45 minutes + 1 hour 30 minutes cooking

4 spanish onions

4 oz (100 g) wholemeal breadcrumbs

1 tablespoon (15 ml spoon) tomato purée

1 teaspoon (5 ml spoon) mixed herbs

4 spring onions, trimmed and chopped

1 oz (25 g) low-fat hard cheese, grated

3 tablespoons (3 × 15 ml spoon) light stock

Oven temperature:
Gas Mark 6/400°F/200°C

Onions are rarely served as a vegetable in their own right. When cooked slowly, a sweet flavour develops which is very different from the sharpness and lingering flavour of raw onion. Use only the large spanish onions for this recipe, because smaller varieties will be too fiddly to handle.

Trim the root end of the onions carefully, and then peel off the brown outer skin from each one. Cook them in boiling water for 1 hour. Remove from the pan using a draining spoon, and rinse under cold water to make them easier to handle. Remove the centre part of the onion, leaving about 2 outer layers, and push through a sieve or put in a food processor. Mix with almost all the breadcrumbs, the tomato purée, the herbs and the spring onions. Stuff the mixture back into the onions, and stand them in an ovenproof dish. Sprinkle them with the remaining breadcrumbs and the cheese. Pour the stock into the bottom of the dish, cover, and bake for 30 minutes, removing the cover for the last 5 minutes to crisp the top.

CHICK PEA PURÉE

One serving has 150 kilocalories and 3 g fat   Serves 6

Preparation time 15 minutes + soaking overnight and 1 hour 30 minutes cooking

2 × 15.2 oz (432 g) can of chick-peas, or 8 oz dried chick-peas

2 cloves of garlic, peeled

1 medium-size onion, peeled and quartered

5.29 oz (150 g) carton of natural yogurt

1 tablespoon (15 ml spoon) chopped parsley

An easy and flavourful alternative to creamed potatoes. Canned chick-peas are more expensive, but save cooking time and fuel. Other beans could be used instead of chick-peas, for instance borlotti or red kidney beans give a good result. Different flavourings can be used to complement the rest of the meal.

If using dried chick-peas, soak them overnight. Rinse them thoroughly and place them in a pan with fresh water. Bring them to the boil, and boil rapidly, covered, for 10 minutes, then simmer for 1¼–1½ hours until tender. If using canned chick-peas, first heat them in a small pan for a few minutes. Drain the chick-peas, reserving the liquid, then either liquidise or put them through a food processor with the garlic, onion and yogurt. Use some of the cooking water, or the liquid from the can, to make a softish purée. Sprinkle the purée with parsley before serving.

CHICK-PEA CURRY

One serving has 210 kilocalories and 3 g fat   Serves 6

Preparation time 5 minutes + soaking overnight + 1 hour 30 minutes cooking

12 oz (375 g) chick-peas

½ teaspoon (2.5 ml spoon) bicarbonate of soda

1 large onion, peeled and quartered

4 cloves of garlic, peeled

1-inch (2.5 cm) piece of root ginger, peeled

This vegetable curry makes an excellent accompaniment to plainly grilled meat or fish but is also very good served with boiled brown rice or with Indian bread like naan or puri. It keeps well for 2–3 days in a refrigerator. In fact the flavour improves and matures after one day.

Soak the chick-peas with the bicarbonate of soda in plenty of water overnight. Drain and rinse. Cover with fresh water and bring to the boil,

8 oz (227 g) can of tomatoes	boil rapidly for 10 minutes then allow to simmer until cooked but not soft (about 1 hour). Drain the chick-peas, and then put all the other ingredients in a liquidiser or food processor and whizz until they are amalgamated. Mix the chick-peas with the curry sauce in a saucepan. Cover the pan, and simmer for 30 minutes. Pour into a serving bowl and garnish with coriander leaves.
1 green chilli, de-seeded	
2 teaspoons (2 × 5 ml spoon) ground cumin	
3 teaspoons (3 × 5 ml spoon) ground coriander	
1 teaspoon (5 ml spoon) paprika pepper	
juice of 1 lemon	

To garnish:

a few coriander leaves

CRISPY BEAN LAYER

One serving has 265 kilocalories and 3 g fat   Serves 6

Preparation time 5 minutes + soaking overnight + 1 hour 30 minutes cooking

6 oz (175 g) red kidney beans

6 oz (175 g) black-eyed beans

6 oz (175 g) mung beans

½ pint (300 ml) tomato juice

1 medium-size onion, chopped very finely

2 cloves of garlic, crushed

2 tablespoons (2 × 15 ml spoon) chopped parsley

4 oz (100 g) fresh wholemeal breadcrumbs

2 oz (50 g) low-fat hard cheese, grated

ground black pepper

Oven temperature:
Gas Mark 5/375°F/190°C

This vegetable dish is really a main course in its own right and would be suitable for vegetarians. Other beans, such as haricot, cannellini, flageolet or butter beans could be used, but keep a contrast in colour between the three layers.

Soak each type of bean separately overnight. Drain and cook each separately in plenty of water. (Pressure cooker dividers are very useful for this so that only one pan need be used.) Bring beans to the boil and boil rapidly for 10 minutes then simmer for 1 hour. Drain. Put in three layers in a large 3-pint (2-litre) ovenproof dish. In a jug, mix the tomato juice, onion, garlic, parsley and pepper and pour them over the beans. Mix the breadcrumbs and cheese, sprinkle these on the top, and bake for 30 minutes.

LAYERED GAZPACHO SALAD

One serving has 35 kilocalories and less than 1 g fat Serves 6

Preparation time 15 minutes

half an iceberg lettuce, shredded

12 oz (350 g) firm tomatoes, skinned

1 cucumber, sliced thinly

2 green peppers or one green and one red pepper, de-seeded and chopped coarsely

¼ pint (150 ml) tomato juice

1 tablespoon (15 ml spoon) red wine vinegar

2 cloves of garlic, crushed

freshly ground black pepper

a few drops of Tabasco sauce

To get the best effect, use a straight-sided glass bowl for this salad, which is a variation on the English summer salad of lettuce, tomato and cucumber. Those who are not on a strict low-fat diet could add a handful of croûtons to their portion.

Put the lettuce in a layer in the bottom of the bowl. Slice the tomatoes and arrange them on top, then do the same with the cucumber and finally the peppers.

Combine the tomato juice, vinegar and garlic. Season the dressing to taste, and pour over the salad at the last minute.

Sweet Pepper Flan

Layered Gazpacho Salad

Spiced White Cabbage

SWEET PEPPER FLAN

One serving has 195 kilocalories and 10 g fat   Serves 6

Preparation time 15 minutes + 20–25 minutes baking

For the pastry:

2 oz (50 g) polyunsaturated
margarine

4 oz (100 g) wholemeal
flour

2 tablespoons (2 × 15 ml
spoon) cold water

For the filling:

2 tablespoons (2 × 15 ml
spoon) corn oil

2 medium-size onions,
peeled and sliced

2 cloves of garlic, peeled and
crushed

2 green peppers, de-seeded
and sliced

1 red pepper, de-seeded and
sliced

1 tablespoon (15 ml spoon)
tomato purée

To garnish:

shredded lettuce (optional)

Oven temperature:
Gas Mark 5/375°F/190°C

The filling of the flan is rather like ratatouille, the Provençal vegetable dish. The flavour of the wholemeal pastry is robust enough to complement the vegetables rather than be masked by them.

Preheat the oven. Make the pastry by rubbing the margarine into the flour, and adding enough cold water to make a firm dough (or use a mixer or food processor). Roll out into a circle, and use to line an 8-inch (20 cm) flan dish. Bake blind for 20–25 minutes. Heat the oil in a pan, and soften the onions and garlic, without browning. Add the sliced peppers and tomato purée. Cover the pan, and simmer for 15 minutes. Pour into the flan case and serve hot, surrounded with shredded lettuce if you like.

SPICED WHITE CABBAGE

One serving has 43 kilocalories and less than 1 g fat   Serves 6

Preparation time 15 minutes

3 tablespoons (3 × 15 ml
spoon) light stock

12 juniper berries, crushed

The texture of the vegetables should still be really crisp, and the colour bright, after cooking. The cabbage can be served either hot or cold, as an accompaniment to any meat or fish.

1 green chilli, de-seeded and chopped

1 lb (450 g) white cabbage, shredded

1 green pepper, de-seeded and shredded

1 red pepper, de-seeded and shredded

2 tablespoons (2 × 15 ml spoon) soy sauce

2 tablespoons (2 × 15 ml spoon) white wine vinegar

1 tablespoon (15 ml spoon) caster sugar

Heat the stock, juniper berries and chilli in a pan, and when they are hot add the cabbage and peppers. Stir over a high heat for 2 minutes, and then add the remaining ingredients. Stir again for a further minute and serve.

LENTILS WALDORF-STYLE

One serving has 325 kilocalories and 5 g fat   Serves 6

Preparation time 15 minutes + soaking overnight + 1 hour cooking

1 lb (450 g) brown lentils

4 sticks of celery, finely sliced

2 oz (50 g) walnut pieces, chopped

3 Cox's apples, quartered, cored and diced

juice of 1 lemon

1 tablespoon (15 ml spoon) Meaux or grainy mustard

To garnish:

chopped parsley

A vegetable dish which would be equally delicious on its own or as an accompaniment to roast or grilled meats. The celery, nuts and apples add a crisp texture and the mustard adds a hint of sharpness to the taste.

Soak the lentils overnight, then drain them and cover them with fresh water in a pan. Bring them to the boil and simmer until they are soft, about 1 hour. Drain the lentils, reserving the water. Put the celery, walnuts, apples and lemon juice in a basin. Drain some of the hot liquid from the lentils into the basin to cover. Liquidise or process the lentils, adding cooking liquid if necessary, to make a thick purée. Drain the liquid from the basin and add the celery, nuts and apple to the purée. Stir in the mustard. Transfer to a warmed serving bowl and garnish with chopped parsley.

DESSERTS, CAKES AND BAKING

The best desserts for healthy eating are fresh fruit, compôtes of dried fruit, and low-fat fruit or natural yogurts, of which a wide range including a feature of the month are available from Sainsbury's. For the occasions when you want something more eye-catching, however, these desserts provide a selection of healthy treats. It is better to get out of the habit of eating between meals, but good bread is a nutritional 'must', and when you really need or long for some other kind of home-baking, turn to these cake and biscuit recipes, for high-fibre, low-fat baking ideas.

Marbled Apricot Cheese

Marinated Fruit Salad

Figgy
Muffins

MARINATED FRUIT SALAD

One serving has 90 kilocalories and negligible fat | Serves 6

Preparation time 20 minutes + 1–2 days marinating

2 peaches, peeled, stoned and sliced

1 pineapple, peeled and diced

8 oz (225 g) strawberries, hulled and sliced if large

8 oz (225 g) blueberries

8 oz (225 g) apricots, halved and stoned

8 oz (225 g) green grapes, halved and de-seeded

grated rind and juice of 2 limes

2 tablespoons (2 × 15 ml spoon) chopped mint

¼ pint (150 ml) sweet white wine, such as Sauternes or Muscat de Beaumes de Venise

This must be made in the summer, however, the fruit can be varied according to what is in season each month. The refrigeration and the mint flavour make it a very refreshing dessert for hot weather.

Layer the six prepared fruits in a glass or china bowl, or preferably in a preserving jar. Make sure each layer contrasts in colour to those adjacent. Mix the lime rind and juice with the mint and wine. Pour this over the fruit and seal tightly. Refrigerate for 1–2 days. Transfer the salad to a serving bowl if you wish, when you want to eat it.

MARBLED APRICOT CHEESE

One serving has 125 kilocalories and negligible fat | Serves 6

Preparation time 30 minutes + soaking overnight

8 oz (225 g) dried apricots

¼ pint (150 ml) unsweetened orange juice

7 oz (200 g) jar of fromage frais with apricots

Apricots are really versatile fruit. They blend well with both sweet and savoury ingredients, and besides this, have a high fibre content. In this dish, the tartness of the purée blends well with the 'creaminess' of the fromage frais, to make a dessert which tastes as if it were really rich – you will need only a small helping!

Soak the apricots with the orange juice for at least 4 hours, or preferably overnight. Bring to the boil, then simmer gently for 15 minutes. Purée the apricots in a liquidiser or food processor, and leave them to cool. Put the fromage frais in a 1-pint (600 ml) serving dish. Spoon in the purée and blend in until marbled but not mixed thoroughly. Serve chilled.

FIGGY MUFFINS

One muffin has 130 kilocalories and 5 g fat	Makes 12

Preparation time 15–20 minutes + 25 minutes baking

4 oz (100 g) wholemeal flour

2 teaspoons (2 × 5 ml spoon) baking powder

3 oz (75 g) bran

1 oz (25 g) soft brown sugar

4 oz (100 g) dried figs, de-stalked and chopped

½ pint (300 ml) skimmed milk

1 small egg (size 4)

3 tablespoons (3 × 15 ml spoon) corn oil, plus extra for greasing

Oven temperature:
Gas Mark 6/400°F/200°C

These are American-style muffins and would be eaten at breakfast in the States. They have a high fibre content and the seeds in the figs give them a delicious crunchy texture. The muffins are nicest served warm.

Sieve the flour and baking powder into a bowl. Stir in the bran, sugar and chopped figs. Mix the liquid ingredients together and pour into the bowl. Stir well and divide the mixture between 12 well-oiled, deep patty tins. Bake for about 25 minutes.

BERRY WHIP

One serving has 90 kilocalories and 1 g fat · Serves 6

Preparation time 10 minutes + chilling

7½ oz (213 g) can of
blackberries in natural juice

15 fl oz (450 ml) carton of
Fruits of the forest yogurt

2 egg whites

*Nothing could be more simply prepared than this dish.
Blackberries have a high fibre content to recommend
them, as well as their delicious autumnal flavour.
Fresh blackberries or any other fresh, soft fruit can be
used in season.*

Drain the juice from the blackberries. Swirl the
fruit and the yogurt together and chill for at least
30 minutes. Just before serving, whisk the egg
whites stiffly and fold them in. Divide between
six bowls.

Passion-fruit Ice Cream

Berry Whip

Selkirk Bannocks

PASSION-FRUIT ICE CREAM

One serving has 110 kilocalories and negligible fat   Serves 4

Preparation time 15 minutes + freezing

½ oz (15 g) custard powder

½ pint (300 ml) skimmed milk

2 oz (50 g) caster sugar

2 passion-fruit

Passion-fruit have a very pronounced flavour which comes through well here. Because of its relatively high water content, this ice cream will need thorough beating at the slushy stage, to break up any ice crystals.

Blend the custard powder with half the milk, bring to the boil, and remove from the heat. Whisk in the remaining milk and sugar. Halve each passion-fruit and remove the flesh and pips. Mix these to a pulp, stir into the ice cream mixture and allow to cool. Pour into a freezer-proof bowl and freeze for about 1 hour until pulpy. Beat again, preferably in a food processor and refreeze for 3–4 hours.

SELKIRK BANNOCKS

One serving has 215 kilocalories and 5 g fat   Makes 2 large bannocks, enough for 8 portions

Preparation time 35 minutes + rising + 30 minutes baking

2 oz (50 g) polyunsaturated margarine

¼ pint (150 ml) skimmed milk

2 teaspoons (2 × 5 ml spoon) dried yeast

2 oz (50 g) soft brown sugar

8 oz (225 g) plain flour

4 oz (100 g) sultanas

Oven temperatures:
Gas Mark 7/425°F/220°C
Gas Mark 5/375°F/190°C

The Scots are excellent at baking, and when I'm in Scotland it's always a delight to me to see their cake shops. The recipe and method below is fairly traditional, but I have also made these bannocks with a packet of white bread mix, mixed with skimmed milk, extra sugar and sultanas. The method is quicker, as the bannocks can be shaped after the first kneading. After spending 5 minutes kneading the dough, you have earned the extra calories!

Warm the margarine and milk to body heat in a small pan, and pour onto the yeast in a small bowl. Stir in 1 teaspoon (5 ml spoon) of the sugar, and leave in a warm place until frothy, about 10 minutes. Sieve the flour into a warmed bowl and stir in the remaining sugar and sultanas. Add the liquid and knead the dough for 5 minutes. Leave to rise, covered with a damp cloth or polythene, in a warm place until doubled in size, about 1 hour. Knead the dough again and divide it into two. Shape each piece into a circle and put on an oiled baking tray. Leave them to rise again in a warm place, for about 20 minutes. Preheat the oven to the higher temperature. Bake for 15 minutes, then reduce the heat to the lower setting for a further 15–20 minutes. Test by tapping the base, which should sound hollow. Cool the bannocks on a wire tray.

SAVOURY PEPPER BREAD

One loaf contains 1898 kilocalories and 17 g fat

Preparation time 20 minutes + rising + 1 hour baking

8 oz (225 g) strong white flour

8 oz (225 g) wheatmeal flour

1 teaspoon (5 ml spoon) coarsely ground black pepper

1 teaspoon (5 ml spoon) mixed herbs

2 teaspoons (2 × 5 ml spoon) dried yeast

1 teaspoon (5 ml spoon) sugar

½ pint (300 ml) skimmed milk, warmed

2 oz (50 g) low-fat hard cheese, grated

oil, for greasing

Oven temperatures:
Gas Mark 7/425°F/220°C
Gas Mark 4/350°F/180°C

The addition of lots of black pepper gives this bread a real bite, while the cheese and herbs give a subtle flavour. The bread is suitable for serving with soups or it can be sliced and used for sandwiches or toast.

Mix the two flours in a large bowl with the pepper and herbs. Mix the yeast and sugar in a basin and pour in the warm milk. Leave for 10 minutes. Pour the contents of the basin into the bowl. Mix it in well, and knead the dough for 3–4 minutes. Add a little warm water if more liquid is needed. Cover the dough loosely with clingfilm and put it in a warm place until it has doubled in size. Add the grated cheese and knead again until smooth. Transfer to an oiled 2 lb (1 kg) loaf tin. Cover the tin and leave to rise for 30 minutes in a warm place. Preheat the oven. Bake at the higher setting for 15 minutes. Reduce heat to the lower setting and bake for a further 45 minutes. Turn out, and cool on a rack.

CURRY OATCAKES

One oatcake has 65 kilocalories and 3 g fat   Makes 24

Preparation time 30 minutes + 15 minutes baking

3 oz (75 g) plain flour

a good pinch of bicarbonate of soda

2 teaspoons (2 × 5 ml spoon) curry powder

8 oz (225 g) medium oatmeal

2 oz (50 g) polyunsaturated margarine

scant ¼ pint (150 ml) hot water

Oven temperature:
Gas Mark 7/425°F/220°C

Do make sure you get the right sort of oatmeal for these biscuits, as porridge oats are not suitable: medium oatmeal is available from health food stores. If you don't like the curry flavour, simple leave the curry powder out. The oatcakes are best with a savoury topping, or with a low-fat cheese.

Sieve the flour, soda and curry powder into a bowl. Stir in the oatmeal. Heat the margarine and water until almost boiling, and add it to the bowl gradually, until the dough is soft but not sticky. Sprinkle the working surface with more oatmeal and roll the dough out thinly. Cut into 3-inch (7.5 cm) diameter rounds. Bake on ungreased tins for 15 minutes. Cool on a wire rack.

POTATO SCONES

One scone has about 80 kilocalories and 4 g fat   Makes about 12

Preparation time 40 minutes + 20 minutes baking

1 lb (450 g) old potatoes, peeled

1 oz (25 g) polyunsaturated margarine

3–4 oz (75–100 g) wholemeal flour

a little oil for brushing the pan

The best varieties of potatoes to use for these scones are King Edwards or Maris Pipers, both of which give a floury texture when boiled. Peel the potatoes as thinly as possible to retain the nutrients stored close to the surface.

Boil the potatoes for about 20 minutes, drain very well, then mash them. It is best to use a sieve or a ricer. Take care if you use a food processor as potatoes quickly go glutinous. Add the margarine while they are still hot, and work in enough flour to make a stiff dough. Roll out on a floured surface to ½-inch (1.25 cm) thick and cut into rounds with a pastry cutter. Brush a heavy frying pan with oil and cook the scones over a medium heat for 5 minutes on each side. Serve while still warm.

STRAWBERRY ROLL

One serving has 180 kilocalories and 2 g fat   Serves 8

Preparation time 20 minutes + 8 minutes baking

3 eggs

4 oz (100 g) caster sugar

4 oz (100 g) plain flour

*1 tablespoon (15 ml spoon)
hot water*

*7 oz (200 g) jar of fromage
frais with strawberries*

*8 oz (225 g) fresh
strawberries, or 14½ oz
(411 g) can of strawberries
in natural juice, drained*

Oven temperature:
Gas Mark 7/425°F/220°C

*This is an absolute indulgence. The sponge roll is
made without fat but there is a little in the egg yolks.
The filling tastes as though it should be really rich, but
it is, in fact, very low in fat. Save this for a treat.*

Line a 14 × 10-inch (35 × 25 cm) swiss roll tin
with greaseproof or silicone paper. Whisk the
eggs and sugar in a large bowl over hot water
until pale and thick. Sieve the flour and fold it
into the eggs, with the hot water. Pour into the
tin and bake for 8 minutes, until golden and set.
Turn out onto a sheet of greaseproof paper on a
clean, damp tea-towel. Peel off the lining paper
and roll the sponge up tightly with the greaseproof paper inside (see diagram). Keep it rolled
up until cool, then unroll it carefully, and spread
it with strawberry fromage frais. Roll the
sponge up again and trim the ends. Purée the
strawberries, and serve them as a sauce with the
roll.

BRAN AND RAISIN LOAF

One slice has 140 kilocalories and 3 g fat — Makes 16 slices

Preparation time 5 minutes + soaking overnight + 1–1¼ hours baking

3 oz (75 g) bran cereal

8 oz (225 g) raisins

6 oz (175 g) soft brown sugar

1 tablespoon (15 ml spoon) orange marmalade

½ pint (300 ml) skimmed milk

6 oz (175 g) self-raising flour

1 teaspoon (5 ml spoon) baking powder

oil, for greasing

Oven temperature:
Gas Mark 5/375°F/190°C

When using bran in cake mixtures, extra raising agent is needed, but the results are delicious and healthy. This loaf will keep well in an airtight tin. Try slices on their own to appreciate the full flavour, but if you like a spread, try skimmed milk soft cheese as a delicious and unusual alternative to margarine.

Mix the cereal, raisins, sugar, marmalade and milk in a bowl and leave to soak for at least 4 hours, and preferably overnight. Oil a 2 lb (1 kg) loaf tin, and line the base with greaseproof paper. Sieve the flour and baking powder into the mixture and mix them in. Pour the batter into the loaf tin and bake for 1–1¼ hours. The loaf is cooked when a skewer inserted in the middle comes out clean. Turn out onto a wire rack and peel off the greaseproof paper. The loaf is best served cold and improves if stored for a couple of days.

INDEX TO RECIPES

Design and layout: Ken Vail Graphic Design
Photography: Laurie Evans
Stylist: Lesley Richardson
Food preparation for photography: Michelle Thomson (pages 4 and 5: Jacki Baxter)
Illustrations: Richard Jacobs
Typesetting: Westholme Graphics Ltd